CW01238265

The Wolf of Gubbio

A Comedy in Three Acts

By Josephine Preston Peabody

(*Mrs. Lionel Marks*)

BOSTON and NEW YORK
HOUGHTON MIFFLIN COMPANY
The Riverside Press Cambridge
1913

TO
LIONEL MY LITTLE SON
AND
LIONEL HIS FATHER

PERSONS OF THE PLAY

THE WOLF
FRANCIS OF ASSISI
BROTHER LEO } *His companions*
BROTHER JUNIPER
NICOLO, the Inn-keeper
LUCIA, his daughter
THE BAKER
THE POTTER
THE FURRIER
THE FURRIER'S WIFE } *People of Gubbio*
THE DYER
THE DYER'S WIFE
OLD LUCREZIA
BIMBO } Children
BIMBA
LOUIS, the King of France
GRILLO } *Two Thieves*
VECCHIO VECCHIO

Persons of the Play

A Poor Man, Giuseppe
A Poor Woman, Assunta   *From Foligno*
And A Baby
Three Dryads

      Other folk of Gubbio.

Time: The day before Christmas, 700 years ago
Place: Italy; in and near Gubbio

  The action falls within the space of twelve hours.

Act I. — *Morning: The woods on the mountain*
Act II. — *Noon: Gubbio*
Act III. — *Night: Gubbio*

Prologue

'*San Francesco!*
San Francesco!
—D'Assisi!
—D'Assisi!
—D'Assisi!'

*The Little Poor Man walked the world.
   (Laugh, laugh, my scars!)
Hunger and thirst, and lack, and loss,
   Beckoned to him as stars.*

. . .

The Wolf of Gubbio

Act I

SCENE: *A deep pine-wood on the mountain. The scene is framed right and left with two towering pine-boles like pillars, front, that reach out of sight without show of green. At the back, a bridle-path crosses; and the clearing, centre, shows a glimpse of the valley far below, with a sweep of silver-bright winter sky. The ground is strewn with coppery pine-needles and dead leaves; a few patches of snow. The dense pines tower out of sight, copper and dun, and laced with greenish light, but few boughs low enough to see. Down, towards the centre, to the left of the spectator, a gray rock, half-covered with pine-needles, shelters the opening of a low cave. Out of the bleak refrain of the wind comes the voice of* THE WOLF, *big and sorrowful.*

4 The Wolf of Gubbio

Voice of The Wolf

THE World is cold; the World is cold.
The snows are round us, fold on fold.
Only the flocks are stalled within;
The kine are gathered, kith and kin.
        . . . I must be growing old.

[*The voice dies away with a moan*]

[A PINE-DRYAD *leans down swayingly from behind the trees in the foreground to the right. A second does likewise, left. Their auburn hair is long and straight; their hanging drapery is filmy green. They beckon each other, and listen, with finger on lip.*]

Voice of The Wolf

Their breath goes up, from stall and pen,
Close beside the homes of men
Gathered together, down below;
Homes of the men of Gubbio.
I have seen their breath float up together,
Warm and white, white as a feather,—
All together, against the cold.
        . . . I must be growing old.

THE WOLF OF GUBBIO

FIRST DRYAD
Who is it? — Did you hear?

SECOND DRYAD
. . . Did you?

VOICE OF A WOOD-DOVE
[*bubblingly*]
Who? . . . Who?

VOICE OF THE WOLF
This old unhappy heart
Does nought to keep me warm.
Dreams come, to vex me in a swarm.
I can but crouch and nurse the smart;
I can but ail, and lie apart,
And hide, from storm to storm.
Watching the little lights below;
Lights, for the men of Gubbio!
The world is very old.
     —And I am cold.

[*The* VINE-DRYAD *appears over the edge of the cliff at back, reaching her way with long arms, from a tree-top just visible. She has dark hair in tendrils; and a garment of green and violet. She listens like the others.*

6 THE WOLF OF GUBBIO

SECOND DRYAD

Hush, can it be?

FIRST DRYAD

... Ah, listen, do!

WOOD-DOVE

Who? ... Who?

VINE-DRYAD

Good-morning, Beautiful!—And happy meeting.

FIRST DRYAD

—Ehi, greeting!

SECOND DRYAD

—Greeting!

VINE-DRYAD

We're listening.

SECOND DRYAD

So am I!
But who?

THE WOLF OF GUBBIO

FIRST DRYAD

And why?
None of you tiptoe Vines could ever guess.—
Some one is pining of his loneliness!

PINE-DRYADS
[*laughing*]

The Wolf— the Wolf it is, — old hulking
    surly—

VINE-DRYAD

Only the Wolf? that woke us all so early?
[*Shivering*]
Oimè!— O Tramontana, change your tune;—
    Let it be June!
[*Joining the others*]

SECOND DRYAD

Hush! We may bring him out, with all this
    patter.

VINE-DRYAD '

Not we, indeed! And if we did, what mat-
    ter?
He has no ears for chatter!

8 THE WOLF OF GUBBIO

FIRST DRYAD

Nor many teeth, by this, for punishment: —
Dull wits, and duller scent.

VINE-DRYAD

There's something in his heart, though, did
 you hear?

WOOD-DOVE

... Fear ... Fear!

FIRST DRYAD
[*looking up in the trees*]

Squirrel, what is it?
Do you find out. Run in, run in and visit!
  [*There are heard and seen little scurryings
  in the dead leaves.*

SECOND DRYAD

Not he! Not he! He knows what he's about.
— Wolf with a secret!

VINE-DRYAD

— Ah, his heavy heart;
No wonder! He must stay with it, you know,
Sulking apart;
  [*A doglike groan from* THE WOLF]
Only his black heart keeping him awake.

The Wolf of Gubbio

First Dryad

For old times' sake!

Vine-Dryad

If I look in to comfort him? — Would you?

Wood-Dove

    Do ... Do!

Second Dryad

Comfort the Wolf? — Ah, hark! —
That sharpens his old fangs along my bark? —
A Wolf that only dreams of bite and
    sup? —
That lives to eat things up!
If I were not a tree,
What hope for me?
You wildest Vine, you runaway romancer!
Creep in and bring an answer!

Vine-Dryad

Hey, rabbit, rabbit, rabbit! Pretty fel-
    low, —
Fratello, fratello! ...
    [*She catches up a hare from his ambush*]

Nestle and fret? And nestle? Ah, don't worry!
I'll let you go — no need of all this flurry.
   Be off, then, — hurry, hurry!
 [*Running and laughing, she throws him softly
  off, left.*
— And I, with you!

    Second Dryad
  Wait, wait! Perhaps he'll tell.

    Vine-Dryad
  [*going blithely*]
       . . . Farewell!
Only a morning dream.

    Second Dryad
   . . . A morning lost!

    First Dryad
My eyes are dim with frost!
 [The Wolf *moans, full diapason. They stop
  and listen, all.*

    Second Dryad
Hush — hush —

The Wolf of Gubbio II

First Dryad
Hush!

Voice of The Wolf
The world is cold,
The world is dark.
Alone I wait; alone I hark.
And hear my own heart grieve:
My sorrow, that no eyes behold;
My longing, longing, sevenfold,
That no one would believe, —
No one would believe.

. . . . .

First Dryad
Sorrow? Believe!

Vine-Dryad
Believe? Not I!   [*Going.*

. . . .

Good-bye!

Second Dryad
Good-bye! . . . Believe? Ahaì, who could!

First Dryad
[*ascending to her tree*]

Hush! Footsteps . . . yonder in the wood.
What if he hear?

Second Dryad

                He never could: —
He's wrapped about with woes!

First Dryad
[*gleefully*]

All, all alone! — Misunderstood, —
Ailing!

Second Dryad

— Or deaf. Who knows?

First Dryad

       . . . . . Or fallen in a doze.
[*They withdraw into their trees and disappear*]
  [*A bell sounds softly, far down in Gubbio.*
  The Wolf *appears at the door of his cave,*
  yawning.

The Wolf

W-wuff! . . . . .
  [*He lifts his nose high in the air*]

The Wolf of Gubbio

Not for fire; and not for war.
What do they sound the great bell for?
Warm, . . . softly, it calls below,
Calling the men of Gubbio.
      [The bell sounds dimly]
I . . . that was master of all the Pack
To ail, and sulk here, — and look back!
I, that could rend, and claw, and grip, —
Sucking my paws, for fellowship!
Puzzling here in my ambuscade,
What men are, when they 're not afraid!
Worrying, — wondering, how 't would feel
To sit with men, and to share their meal;
Talking words, with my bite and sup
Out of a man-made, earthen cup . . .
      [The bell sounds again]
Talking words, when the north wind blows,
Round the fire, . . . with nose to nose.
      [complacently]
I was a tempest and a woe,
Unto the men of Gubbio . . .
Only one thing men do full well; —
How did they make . . . the bell?
  [A running is heard through the dry leaves]
. . . W-ufff . . .
[THE WOLF *withdraws his head into the cave*]

[*Enter right, two children,* BIMBO *and* BIMBA, *breathless. They run stumblingly close by* THE WOLF'S *cave, in manifest terror and out of their way.*]

BIMBA

— Stop, stop! I have no breath.

PINE-DRYADS
[*softly from above*]

... Away .... away.

[*The children look up at trees, but see nothing.* BIMBO *takes out his pocket-knife, scared and at bay. They huddle together, panting out their words.*]

BIMBA

What was that? —

BIMBO

Wind, wind, — Tramontana! — Come, run, run!

BIMBA
[*sobbingly*]

I can't run any more. I can't run any more. No, no! not if I saw the Wolf himself...

I could n't run any more! [*A slight contemptuous sniff is heard from the cave.*] Oh, what was that?

Bimbo
[*with chattering teeth*]

. . . Tramontana! — Ssh! — They 'll find us.

Bimba

Oh! oh! — And she called us to find the baby . . . she begged us to find the baby. I don't dare. I don't dare!

Bimbo

We did n't see any baby. How could we find any baby? What's that? — [*A cone falls.*

Bimba
[*looking up at the tree with a tear-stained smile*]

Tramontana blew us something down, out of the pine-tree!

Bimbo

Come on, come on! . . . We 'll catch it at home too. Spilling all the firewood. . . . Oh! [*Stops.*] They 're coming. They 're after us!

Bimba

Get under the leaves. — Get under the leaves! And if he comes near, we'll make-believe we're rabbits. — Get under the leaves!

[*They burrow head-first under the leaves. Enter up right, on the path, Brother Juniper, a simple peasant Friar Minor,— with a look of constant anxiety illumined by beaming good will. He leads a donkey laden with faggots; and he is followed by Brother Leo, slim and young. Brother Juniper turns towards the rustling leaves. The burrowing children are wild with terror.*

Bimba

[*in a little high voice as he approaches*]

Oh, please . . . I'm only a rabbit . . . Oh, Messer Robber. . . . It isn't anything but a fox, a . . . a little fox . . . a *little, little* fox!

Juniper

[*calling back to Leo as he approaches*]

Fra Leo, Fra Leo, — come here, for love of Our Lady! I have found a heap of leaves that is bewitched; and calling out, — how it is now a fox, and now a rabbit, . . . and now, it is [BIMBA *crawls out gladly*] a child, — a very child, a woman-child, — as I am Brother Juniper, the silly plaything of the blessed saints!

LEO
[*sweetly to her*]

Give thee peace, little child. Was this the sorrowing we heard? [BIMBO *crawls out.*

JUNIPER

Another! And is it a rabbit enchanted you are, or a boy bewitched, in God's name? And whence was the crying?

BIMBA

O Brother Juniper, take us home, come with us — quick, quick! We thought you were Men.

BIMBO

Robbers!

JUNIPER *and* LEO

— Robbers? — [*Pointing back.*

BIMBA

We came all the way from Gubbio —

BIMBO

Gathering wood. Blessed Francis was coming to Gubbio.

BIMBA

— This day! to make the Christmas feast for us. — And we went farther and farther. And we heard a crying —

BIMBO

— And there was a woman —

BIMBA

— Striving with a man — and calling out to us to find the Baby.

BIMBO

We did n't see any baby. . . .

BIMBA

— And we did n't dare. And she called to us . . . how it was under a juniper-tree.

Bimbo

—No, an olive-tree.

Bimba

—No, a juniper-tree. But we durst n't—
... we were frightened. ... We ran ...
[*Shivering.*
[Leo *unbinds his hood and puts it on the
little girl.*

Bimbo

Of course we ran! And we must run home now. There's the way. [*Pointing left.*

Leo

Alas, poor woman! 'T was her crying, then.

Bimba

Oh, please to take us home!

Leo

Yea, little doves, that will we.

Juniper

Even to Gubbio we are all bent this day, to make ready the birthday feast for Our Lord's poor, and the blessed little father Francis is coming fast the way of Monte Subasio.

CHILDREN
[*dancing*]

Little Poor Man, — Little Poor Man!

BIMBA

Is he coming truly? — All this long way in the cold? —

LEO

Yea, little dove, his heart will warm the wind.

BIMBO
[*excitedly gazing at the donkey*]

Eh! Nicolo never lent you Pantaleone! ...

BIMBA

No, it's the bishop's ass! The bishop's ass! He sent it for blessed Francis!

LEO

But blessed Francis goes afoot, all through the world. Moreover, this being the Holy Eve, it ought, as he says, to be a time of gladness for

Brother Ass, — with all God's poor, — and with all God's creatures on two legs, or three or four!

Juniper
[*beating his breast suddenly*]

Mea culpa, what a rogue am I! . . . [*He hastens to the ass and untackles the firewood.*] That set but now this burden on my brother! Who should go freely, honorably, . . even leaping as it were with holy exultation. . (Light down, light down, Brother Wood!) — Yet this once, [*cooingly to the ass*] think it no burden, but a kindness, brother, to take this little one upon you, a child as it were, and for sake of the Holy Child!

[*Takes the wood upon his back,* Fra Leo *helping. They beckon the children.*

Leo

Yea, let us find the poor soul that fell among thieves.

[*Turning right*]

Bimbo

No, this way, this way!

JUNIPER

—And her babe that she left in jeopardy as it were. . . . This winter day! . . . and the wind . . . And the wolves . . .

BIMBO *and* BIMBA

Wolves!

LEO

Which way said she?

  [*The children look at each other guiltily, then point off, left.*

JUNIPER

[*gladly*]

The homeward way?— Come, we will search as we go!

  [*The Brothers lift* BIMBA *on the ass, and they all go out, left, on the bridle-path to Gubbio.*

  THE WOLF *reappears at the door of his cave and sniffs tentatively in the direction pointed out by the children.*

THE WOLF

Hmph!
Wanted to tell . . . but did n't dare.

The Wolf of Gubbio

The little whelps! — No baby there.

  [Yawns and shuffles back in his cave: lies down with his nose out, boredly.

The world goes by,
The world goes by;
Forgotten in my lair I lie.
No, not forgotten; — down below,
I am a name in Gubbio;
I am a dread; though here apart
I nurse the thorn that's in my heart,
Watching the snows that melt, and drip;
Licking my paws, for fellowship!
Wondering what if a man came by,
To stand, to face me, eye for an eye;
Knifeless, fearless — ?
. . . . What would he do?
Ah, — such a man must be. But who?

  [He yawns prodigiously; starts up and gives a low growl; lies down, disappointed, nose on his paws. His subsiding grunts speak boredom and disgust.

Bah! The sound . . . of the smell that grieves: —
Hope, betrayed by a cynic nose!
Just when an old heart half believes . . .

Same old, mouldy odor . . . of thieves!
— May as well doze.

[*Enter up, cautiously,* Vecchio Vecchio, *a tattered but unctuous optimist, and* Grillo, *lean and bitter, with a cloak in his hands.*

Vecchio Vecchio

Come along, Snail!

Grillo

Go along, Ox. — Do you look to go shares on my takings, Lie-Abed-Late? Look at me; he had the muscle of a copper-smith, that fellow. I have got a contortion of the spleen, pitching him over the cliff!

Vecchio Vecchio

Gathering cones, were they? Sooth, they'll be gathering up the bones of him, white as coral, next spring, when the snow in the gorge is melted. — Come, what catch, my limber little fisherman?

[*Grasping his arm*]

Grillo

Softly, Bishop!—And a man of his size, groaning and cursing about his wife and the 'Baby, baby, baby!' . . . As if I were out child-napping.

[*They come down to the rock over* The Wolf, *and cut along the lining of the cloak together.*

Vecchio Vecchio

And the wife, while I searched her, screaming to the fowls of the air to save the 'Baby, baby — baby!'—And all the while, no man required the baby . . . only this poor pittance, or saving,— or inheritance . . Where is it, Sheepshead? sneeze out, I say!

Grillo
[*with a wry face, unfolding a few coins and a small packet*]

Here was a witless woman. With all her struggle and cawing to get away, yielding up her husband to be thrown off the mountain—and her babe mislaid under a tree she will never find again,—she clings to the cloak; and we cling too. [*With disgust.*] Her all-in-all, — her treasury! . . A little bread, less cheese . . . and an image of a woman and a baby.

[*He hastily crosses himself on second thought*]

Vecchio Vecchio

No matter; this snack will stay us. [*Sniffing at it.*] *Peccorino!* The fourth time this week. Bah, — when we have but the coat of that nobleman of France we look to entertain — [*looking off left with concentrated purpose*] that nobleman of France who keeps us waiting, — we shall dine.

Grillo

Per Bacco! 'Tis a rare snail. If he go another way?

Vecchio Vecchio

There is no other way, for a bridle-path!
  [*They scramble upon* The Wolf's *rock, and eat their cheese, watching the path alertly.* Vecchio Vecchio *lifts up the cloak, sniggeringly, and puts it round his shoulders.*

Take off thine evil eye from my rich garment! 'Twas folly to waste us on these small fry, these creatures of Poverty, . . . hee — hee!—The world's failures.—Consider the man;—what a man! Base victim of his own unthrift. Puts all his coin in his wife's hood and loses it; ho—ho! And the woman, lean victim of her own unthrift! Why did she not lay up her hoardings in store of flocks or geese? Sews it all in her cloak for a journey.—Wastrel, to journey at all! Improvident from birth! With a young babe, forsooth; flaunting the swaddled creature to all the winds!— Mislays it under a juniper-tree, —hee—hee! A birthday gift for the Wolf of Gubbio!

> [THE WOLF'S *head appears suddenly, at the opening of his cave. The thieves, sitting above him vis-à-vis, do not perceive it. He sniffs long and earnestly from up centre, to the right as they talk, and listens with a growing interest evident in his red tongue and side-glances.*

Go to; were it not for the chance of its wauling, I would seek out that babe, and bring it up in the fear of folly! Ho—ho! How long must we suffer by this swarm of babes? How is the noble world shamed by this spawning, this seething, this weltering of ill-conditioned babes, like

... cheese-mites; children of fools; — pale victims of their own unthrift! But all's well, or I am no philosopher. All's well: — I had it of a learned man I met . . on the road to Padua.

GRILLO
[*with intense bitterness*]
All's well? — All's rotten: look at me!

VECCHIO VECCHIO
[*waving him aside*]
The woman finds her way back; the better for her. — Or, she finds it not; the better for her kindred. — The man is free to carve his pathway in the world. — [*Flourishing his knife over the cheese.*]

GRILLO
[*with his mouth full*]
— If he live to find it.

VECCHIO VECCHIO
[*his eyes rolled up, piously*]
Freed of his Lawful Encumbrance. — And what more notable goad to valor and industry than the goad of Poverty? — As the lord bishop

was telling you at Foligno, while you fished for his purse —

Grillo

(Ugh! — my rotten luck.)

Vecchio Vecchio

'The goad of Poverty, scourging the slothful and pricking on the poor.'

Grillo
[*with venom*]

Poverty? ... Old Cheese, look at *me*, I tell you, look at me!

Vecchio Vecchio

I look, I look, and I repeat. Wastrels all, scatterlings, — locusts! Fie upon thee to devour thy cheese. Put by, put by, for a rainy day, — while I eat mine, of a chilly! Go to, thou ravening locust! Mark you this (I had it of a doctor I met . . on the road to Bologna): — Nothing will keep you idlers at home, save the fear of the Wolf at the door. Now am I a scholar or —

[The Wolf *scents something, and snaps his jaws suddenly.*

Grillo

Hist! What was that?
 [*He rises and turns towards the bridle-path.*
 The Wolf *listens to their talk with growing animation.*

Vecchio Vecchio

Thou mettlesome thoroughbred!—Peace, peace. Benedicite! Requies-s-scat! ... To continue:—the babe is lost; one less in a crowded world.

Grillo

Nay, go on, Bishop. Thou hast left the babe with the Wolf of Gubbio. ... Hee—hee—hee! The Wolf will keep him warm

Vecchio Vecchio

Thou hast a ribald fancy and a darkened mind. What wolf, finding a babe in the forest of a winter eve, would swallow it down, without a wash of wine? So to misprize it? Never! Nay, devour an orphan babe? He would fetch the creature home, to show him *gratitude;* for why else does a man fetch anything home?—

[*unctuously*] but for something to love him; to be the prop of his declining years!

Grillo

—Clothe it with skins! Teach it Wolf's Latin—

Vecchio Vecchio

And bring it up godly,—to be a brown friar, absolve him of his sins, and sing masses for his departing soul!

[The Wolf, *with a last decisive sniff high in air, darts out noiselessly, right.*

Both

What was that? Hist!

Grillo

'T was a scantling in the leaves . . .

Vecchio Vecchio

A rabbit? . . [*Looking up.*] The day's grown milder.   [*Listening.*

Grillo

Nay, it's there now. [*Pointing left.*] What if he be not alone? . . . My rotten luck!

VECCHIO VECCHIO

Chut!—What's a man or two? You heard him say it with his own mouth, in the courtyard at Foligno,—as we lay behind the wall, ... he would go without escort? And his men-at-arms were to fall away?—*Ib, ib!* An he keep us waiting longer ...

> [*They go up, to look down the bridle-path, and steal to the right on tiptoe, lost to sight for the moment.*
>
> *Reënter down, right,* THE WOLF *in haste, with a bundle like a swaddled Babe in his teeth. He stops, somewhat at a loss,—puts it down among the pine-needles, centre, and goes up on the trail of the two thieves, to reconnoitre.*
>
> THE PINE-DRYADS *unfold from their trees, and lean down, right and left, their long arms almost touching as they droop over the Baby with curiosity and cherishing delight; then watchful looks towards* THE WOLF.
>
> *Appears on the edge of the cliff again,* THE VINE-DRYAD, *reassuring them with a gesture of mirth and wonder, pointing to* THE WOLF, *who is watching the thieves in their covert.*

The Wolf
[*turning*]

Wuff—

[*He wags his tail as he looks at the Baby, and then up, right.* The Dryads *withdraw slowly into the trees.* The Wolf *runs down,— noses the Babe gently, gets it into his teeth again bundle-wise, and creeps into his cave.*

He is seen guardant, his head out, but withdrawn as the two thieves reappear, looking back for their prey. A soft sound comes from the cave.

Grillo
[*startled*]

Hist!—

As I'm a lean sinner, I could swear I heard a sound, as it were of a babe,— a swaddled babe!

Vecchio Vecchio
[*recovering himself*]

A swaddled babe! Thou heardst a sound as of a swaddled babe, with auburn locks, lying under a tree that was planted the year of the death of King Pepin!

Grillo

What was it? — If it be the babe, — we've missed our way; we've rounded on ourselves. We left the woman — [*Pointing back, right.*

Vecchio Vecchio

Peace, dolt! Thou heardst a rabbit calling thee grandmother.

Grillo

— If it be the babe, we are lost through its wauling!

Vecchio Vecchio

If it be a babe, and if we lag, and if it waul, and if we be lost, — we be lost through thy Iff-ings and What-ings, — thou beardless son of an earth-worm. [*Both listen, right.*
— Here he comes, Silver-Trappings! here he comes, with his miniver edgings. Quick — to work!

> [*They run with sudden stealth, to conceal themselves behind the trees up right and left, with knives drawn.*
> *Hoof-beats are heard, of horses walked gently*

THE WOLF OF GUBBIO

on the mountain-path; a jingling of trappings.

The watchers, with faces turned suddenly to deadly rage and disappointment, steal farther down front to concealment, looking back.

GRILLO

Death of my life! Six men-at-arms.

VECCHIO VECCHIO

Blast him, — blast him, the flea of fortune!
Who and what is he?

[*The knights are seen to ride along behind the pine-trees at back. In the centre, up,* LOUIS OF FRANCE *reins his horse and leans from the saddle with boyish eagerness. He is a young and comely man, clothed with knightly richness, but bare-headed.*

LOUIS

Look, there lies Gubbio! When we shall come
To yonder bridge, I go afoot. [*To one.*] . . . René,
Have by the pilgrim robes that I must wear;
[*To the others*]
And when we pass the wall, — no sign from
you.

Think of that holy man I go to meet,
The blessed Francis ! . . . and of heaven's high
    King, —
    [*They bare their heads*]
How lowly to this world he came alone,
A naked Babe. Think ye, within your minds,
As we ride on. For we be pilgrims all
Together, on this Birthday of my Lord,
To keep His feast with holy Poverty. —
Yea, and to pray, as men that be in need,
The Little Poor Man for some blessedness,
The Little Poor Man whom we go to seek !
And when I shall dismount, then do you all
Follow me, at a distance. . Stay me not,
Whatever thing it pleasure me to do.
Ride on, Sirs.
  [*The riders pass out left on the path to Gubbio*]

GRILLO

Would you not take him for a vagrom preaching friar? Curled lap-dog! He journeys like the king of France home from the crusades! 'Ride on, Sirs!' And a pious dog would I be too, if preaching could line my coat with vair and my belly with partridge pies! 'Follow me at a distance, gentlemen!'

The Wolf of Gubbio

Vecchio Vecchio

Pish! If they follow him at a distance as he said, — we shall have the coat, and the vair, with the partridge pies to follow! And a 'little poor man, a little poor man,' he longed to meet? — *Ib, ib,* — so do not I! — Hold thy tongue; and hurry thy heels. For we'll follow him on, to Gubbio.

Grillo

— *Pilgrims all, to Gubbio!*

Vecchio Vecchio

And mark the inn that he lies at. — Follow you 'at a distance,' pretty Sir! Follow you at a distance!

> [*They start after, with venomous looks,* Grillo *first, who stops and waves back* Vecchio Vecchio, *cautioning.*
> *A man's voice is heard singing off, right;*
>   O Brother Sun . . .
>   All-folding Sight!
> [The Wolf, *at the door of his cave, starts up, with sudden eagerness.*

Grillo

What fool is this?

38 THE WOLF OF GUBBIO

VECCHIO VECCHIO

Some wandering simpleton . . . calling to all the winds to come and pluck him. — Pluck him we will; he'll never cry out! — I'm cold.

[*They stand ready. The singing comes nearer*]
[THE WOLF *trembles with excitement and creeps out, watching also.*

THE VOICE OF FRANCIS

O Brother Sun!
All-folding Sight,
Lo, where I sing along the dust!
Even a little one,
Yea, a wayside thing
Sunlight makes to sing, as he must!
All we are minstrels of thy King:
Maker of thy might,
Pouring from above: —
O Light of Light,
O Love of Love!

[*Enter* ST. FRANCIS, *shining with gladness. The thieves run to seize him.* — THE WOLF *utters a furious snarl.*
They loose ST. FRANCIS, *and turn to see* THE WOLF *crouching, ready to spring.*

The Wolf of Gubbio

VECCHIO VECCHIO *and* GRILLO
[mad with fear]
The Wolf of Gubbio! — The Wolf of Gubbio! *[They rush out, left]*
[ST. FRANCIS *stretches out his arms in greeting*]

FRANCIS
. . . Welcome, Brother Wolf!

[THE WOLF *still crouching looks at him. A moment of silence.*

THE WOLF
Brother . . . you called me?

FRANCIS
Even so.

THE WOLF
And Wolf? —

FRANCIS
Yea, . . . truly.

THE WOLF
Then you know. Why are you not dismayed? . . .

The Wolf of Gubbio

Francis

        At thee?
[*He spreads his arms wide, with a gesture of sweet mirth.*
Why art not thou . . . afraid of *me*?

The Wolf
[*with nose abased*]

You have heard them . . . Now you know
All. — You heard them say my name.
Sooth, it had a bitter fame,
Long ago.
I am . . . the Wolf of Gubbio.
There is no more to say.

Francis

        Thou he?
Long, — long have I looked for thee.

The Wolf

Fair Sir, have pity on my shame.

Francis

Shame? — Then you shall tell it me.
Nay, you shall not be afraid.

What am I for? — Your *Poverello*
Out of Assisi, a low little fellow!
These ears of mine were only made
To hear things sorrowful and sore.
    Come, you shall tell me more.
[*He comes down.* THE WOLF *stays between*
    FRANCIS *and the opening to the lair.*

THE WOLF

Wolf I am, from last to first.
Ah, but 'Wolf' is not the worst.
. . . No, I am accurst.

FRANCIS
[*with childlike delight*]

Hearken here; and then believe.
Dost thou know, this Holy Eve,
How the mouth of Brother Ox,
And the ass, — and all the flocks, —
Speak His praise, with one accord,
    Who is made our Lord?
Lord of thee and me, and all;
Kings that sit within the hall, —
Lambs that bleat within the fold;
Yea, and men and wolves that call
    In the cold!

Brother, of thy courtesy,
Lay thy burden here on me;
Give me leave to ease thy smart;
Shew me all thy heart.
[*He lifts one of* The Wolf's *paws in his hands*]

The Wolf

Oh, what is it? What is waking
Here in my old hide?
Sir, my strength is breaking . . .
With my pride.
Is it the noon-day, maybe? — No,
It must be music, ails me so.
It's in my ears. — It warps my gait.
I . . . can't walk straight.

Francis

Tell me thy burden.

The Wolf
[*shamedly*]
    If I can.
I long . . . I long to be a Man.
. . . .
And here am I, a Wolf, behold!
The world's the world. —

The Wolf of Gubbio 4

. . . . And it is cold.
And I am old.
Francis
Brother, I know.
The Wolf
[*trying to recover his self-possession*]
Well, you would hear.— I told you so !
I never thought, when life began,
That one could wish to be a Man.
But — one by one, the Pack died out;—
And nothing much to think about,
Grinding your teeth on one idea;
And little passing here . . .
And sometimes we can hear it well,—
When the wind's right . . . that Bell.
. . . .
So; I have told you. Yet, in spite
Of dreaming on, night after night,—
I've always found, the frosty days
Brought back my wolfish ways. . . .
Sometimes a sheep, — even a cow,
Made me forget, — and break my vow.
Sometimes . . . [*Breaks off.*] Wff . .
Not that I want for bite and sup !
[*Proudly*]
I . . . couldn't keep it up.

Then after all, up here again,
Alone and moping in my den . . .
  [*He steals a guilty look towards it, and searches the face of* St. Francis *for knowledge; then turns his back on his den resolutely and goes on.*
I longed to be with Men;
To be a Man, as others are : —
No, no, — I don't mean similar.
I've never seen nor yet heard tell
Much good of men, — but, well,
Maybe some glamour of romance,
For all this — circumstance ; . . .
  [*Looking round at his tail*]
. . . I'd simply like the chance !

Francis

Ah, Brother mine, a Wolf thou wert
To spread dismay !
Was it not to their mischief and their hurt
To come thy way ?

The Wolf
[*meditating*]
Yea.

The Wolf of Gubbio

Francis
Thy cruelties were more than men could say —

The Wolf
. . . . Yea.

Francis
To make of thee, thyself, this castaway.

The Wolf
[acquiescent]
. . . . Hm-hm̂.

Francis
Ah, dear my Brother, for this cause
Thy hands keep on their savage claws;
And splendor of thy furry hide
Keeps hot thy heart of wolfish pride.
Yea, but thine own heart after all
   Hath made thee thrall:
Keeps thee in pain, bites in on thee
With the sharp tooth of misery.

The Wolf
Thou sayest all.

FRANCIS
Yea, Brother, have I understood?

THE WOLF
I was longing . . . to be good.

FRANCIS
[*blithely*]
Longing lights the lovely fire;
Longing brings thee still no nigher
To thy heart's desire.
Work, and work; and thou shalt know.
Come!

THE WOLF
. . . But where?

FRANCIS
     To Gubbio!
[THE WOLF *starts up; then crouches again and steals a furtive look at his rock considering whether he shall tell.*
[*Buoyantly*]
Where thy plunders stripped thee first;
Where thy teeth have done their worst.

THE WOLF
Oh, I am accurst, — accurst.

FRANCIS

Is there a burden left thee, say?

THE WOLF
[*evading the query*]

Let me be with thee, for one day!
. . . .
Ask no more . . . Ah, if you knew,
Would you not hate me? — even you!

FRANCIS

Hate thee, — I? Ah, Brother, see!
And do thou cry out on me;
A wolf, — a low and little one!
Regard the evil I have done: —
[*He points earnestly to a scrap of fox-skin
   sewn upon the breast of his habit, and goes
   on with pleading eagerness, while* THE
   WOLF *sniffs up and down the patch.*
This bit of fox-fur, — sniff! — behold!
And more, and larger, sewn within,
To warm my sorry little skin
      Against the winter cold! . . .
When Brother Fox was found undone,
I, like a very heathen Hun,

Suffered a portion of his fur
To make my bones the happier!
Yea, of my self-love, so I did;
And this I wear, as thou wilt guess
To show all men my wolfishness,
And not to keep it hid!
> [THE WOLF *struggles with his conscience;
> and encourages himself with his tail.*

FRANCIS

To Gubbio, come!
> [*A sound of running water begins to be heard; sunlight steals through the tree-trunks and warms the sky to gold.*

THE WOLF

They hate me.

FRANCIS

          Wilt thou earn
A man's own peace? Then work, and learn!
Back to the world; and there make good
All thou hast dreamed of brotherhood.
Hope and lose and hope again,
And remember, and forget,

With us all; for men are men,
But not brothers; — no, not yet.

The Wolf

Not brothers yet? Then what's the game?
Surely Men were all the same
       . . . Till you came.

Francis

In this twilight of thy wood! —

The Wolf

I was longing . . . to be good.
    [*Looking back at his den*]

Francis
    [*joyously*]

Work, with each of thy four paws.
Mind thee what thy teeth and claws
Tore from all these village-folk; —
Homes that trembled; hearts that broke.
Work, for those thou hast beguiled; —
Left without or chick or child!
  [The Wolf *flattens himself suddenly*]

THE WOLF
But they hate me. . . .

FRANCIS
Even so,
Come again to Gubbio.

THE WOLF
How can any gladness be?

FRANCIS
Thou shalt see.

THE WOLF
Can you think, and still say Go?

FRANCIS
[*smilingly*]
Nay, but Come;—and come with me!

THE WOLF
[*rising giddily*]
Why . . . is the snow . . . melting along the furrows?
Is it spring?

Why . . . do the hares . . . look out from
their hutches and burrows?
Listening?

FRANCIS

Love in the world it is, that makes all these
Awake and warm: —
Love walking in the world, that all the trees
Forget the storm.

THE WOLF

Why are the vines astir that were forsaken?
Can it be spring?
Why is the brook awake? — I heard it waken.

FRANCIS

And it will sing!
[*seeing* THE WOLF *halt*]
Is there something left behind?
Rankling thorn? — Or prick of mind? —
Shall we two believe each other?

THE WOLF
[*leaping about him with dog-like gaiety*]
Give the word. I will obey!

Francis

Come with me. — Here lies the way,
    Wolf, my Brother!

[He goes radiantly up to the bridle-path and looks down at Gubbio. The Dryads lean from the trees softly: they point towards The Wolf's den with accusing looks.

The Wolf, avoiding their eyes, drags his tail and walks heavily after the Saint, stopping for a last hangdog glance at the cave where the Baby lies hidden. As Francis turns, he waves his tail, and prances after, with every sign of high spirits.

The Wolf
[looking back]

Wf! But shall I? — Would he? . . . No!

Francis
[turning]

Pilgrims all, — to Gubbio!

[They go out together on the path to Gubbio; a sudden troop of wild doves after, like a flurry of snow.

The Wolf of Gubbio

The scene fills with the sound of running water and new-wakening trees. The bird-voices grow to a chorus.

Birds

San Francesco!
San Francesco!
— D'Assisi!
— D'Assisi!
— D'Assisi!

Curtain

The Little Poor Man smiled at me;
His eyes were like the sun.
And down the years, like sunlit tears,
The pouring light did run!

* * *

Act II

Scene: *A market-place in Gubbio: bright afternoon. Right and left, uniform and opposite each other, are stone arcades shading the little house-fronts, with humble wares hanging out, and a few caged blackbirds and pigeons.*
Down, left, nearest the spectators, is The Furrier's; *next,* The Dyer's. *Down, right,* The Potter's *booth and his wheel; then* Old Lucrezia's *doorway. Front, left and right, their walls turn the corners, and show withered leaves hanging on the grape-vines, and weeds in the stone crevices of the walled byway. In the wall to the left, there is a tiny alcove-shrine high up, with a dim terra-cotta relief of the Virgin and Child.*
At the back, a wide arch crosses the scene,— running into a buttressed wall with a fountain, right. Left, it joins a flight of uneven stone steps, that lead, after the manner of Italian hill-towns, to an upper street; of which there is visible only a glimpse of

blue sky, — Nicolo's inn-door, left, and a buttress of the Duomo, right. The archway makes a viaduct over the market-place.

Under the archway is a glimpse of the road, sprinkled with sun and shade; and to the left, directly beneath it, a stable-door.

At rise of the curtain, the people are busied in their doorways (with the exception of Nicolo the inn-keeper); Lucia and other girls are filling their copper water-jars at the fountain by the archway.

Brother Juniper comes down the steps from the upper square, gently leading Assunta, — a worn, Madonna-like young peasant, poorly clad, spent with grief and exhaustion.

Juniper

TAKE heart, poor soul, take heart! . . . And even as Our Lady came to her refuge this day, riding lowly upon an ass, — take comfort and be gently led, so. . . even by me who am less than an ass, — Brother Juniper, a fool among the brothers.

    [*The people hasten towards him with eager greetings, and stand still on recognizing Assunta.*

The People of Gubbio

— Brother Juniper, Brother Juniper!
— Are you here at last?
— Where's the holy Francis?
— And who is this?
> [Assunta *takes her hands from her eyes and looks through them, not at them, stark with grief.*

The Dyer's Wife

The woman of Foligno, back again! — What ever befell you?

The Furrier's Wife

— With your eyes as great as an owl's by daytime, —

Lucia

— And your man, where's he? And the babe?

Juniper

Ah, her man, — her babe! [*Warning them, with a gesture of pity.*] A sorry tale this, sweet brothers ... And no song for her to sing you. Look you, the poor soul is sore spent and out of measure full of woe; and beyond that, oppressed, with singular great sorrow.

> [*A clatter of hoofs, and the donkey appears under the archway, led by* BROTHER LEO, *who carries the firewood on his back, while* BIMBA *and* BIMBO *ride upon the donkey. The women go to meet them.*

THE DYER'S WIFE

Holy Mother! What do I see? The children riding home on the lord bishop's ass that he sent for holy Francis!—Oh where have you been? Where have you been? And I that had forgotten you all the morning, and what you were sent to fetch!—Light down, light down off the lord bishop's ass,—the two little wasps that you are!

LEO

Have patience, lady.

BIMBO *and* BIMBA

—We lost the faggots!
—We heard a thief.—
—We met a robber!

WOMEN

A thief,—a robber!

BIMBA

We heard a loud crying; so we ran —

BIMBO

But we turned to look —

BIMBA *and* BIMBO
[*pointing to* ASSUNTA]

And it was she —

BIMBA

— And an ugly man after her. So we ran away and hid from the noise. And darling Brother Juniper came by and found us; and Brother Leo —

> [ASSUNTA *sits down on the edge of the fountain and shuts her eyes, leaning against the stone archway, heedless of the gossips.*

JUNIPER

Even so, little sheep. And her too we found, [*looking at* ASSUNTA] coming away out of the woods to Gubbio, — spent and fainting. But the babe ... we sought for, even in the place where she had laid it for safe-keeping, under a certain tree; the babe we sought for ... and found not.

> [BROTHER LEO *waters the ass at the fountain, regarding* ASSUNTA *with pity.*
> *Enter above at the top of the steps,* NICOLO, *a robust and voluble man of Gubbio.*

NICOLO
> [*descending*]

— The bishop's ass!

> [BROTHER LEO *leads the ass off under the archway, and returns.*

THE PEOPLE
> [*still staring at* ASSUNTA]

— Found not?
— Why, then it is lost!
— It may be stolen, — stolen by witches.
— Dead of the cold!
— Eaten of wolves!

> [ASSUNTA, *hearing, shudders*]

LEO

Ah, Messer Nicolo, you are the one to help

us. Take her in, for the love of Our Lady. She is perishing of sorrow; — her man gone, her babe —

Bimbo

No, he is n't the one, Nicolo is n't, — not he!

Bimba

— For she was telling us as she came, how he would n't let them stay over the feast of the blessed Nativity; for they had n't brought enough money with them to last, and she could n't walk all the way to Arezzo.

Nicolo

Ah, you magpies! What will you, what will you? — Tell not this to holy Francis! Was I not going, this hour, this minute, what you will, to lay before holy Francis all that I have and more? — The moment I should behold him coming upon the lord bishop's ass? — As to the woman, what will you? Did she not come here three days back, and her man along with her, too? — A potter, he said, — of Foligno!

The Potter
[*with rancor unspeakable*]

Ah, ah, Foligno!—*Foligno, Fossato, Spello?*
—*Pah!*

The Furrier's Wife

—And thinking to come to Arezzo for the holy season, she with a babe of days in her arms!

The Dyer's Wife

—Yes, we all saw it! What a thing! Starting to walk all the way to Arezzo with the babe, and yet unable. Could we help it that she was a weakling?

Nicolo

—Could we help it that she had not wherewith to pay? Marry, why did they set out to walk, then, if they could n't walk?

Leo

Brother, for holy Charity, you are the host of this place. Take her back to the inn; and let us search till we find . . . that which is lost.

Nicolo

But, indeed, Fra Leo, there is no room at the

inn; no room, whatever, in reason, at all; nowise, — none, none! [*With copious indignation.*] Have I not told you all? And did I not, when I sent them off, tell both the two and the babe likewise? And am I not telling you again? — How I was bidden to make all room and preparation for a great nobleman out of France, who is coming this day, and maybe this hour, with his six gentlemen, to sup and to stop and to lie here this night, and who can tell how long after?

Lucia

It's the simple truth we are telling. Six gentlemen with him. — I go to bring fresh water now with my own hands.

Nicolo

We have no room for beggars . . . Nor for any potter from Foligno; nor for his wife; nor to crown all, a swaddled creature of days! wauling day and night! — For what else would it be doing, if I let it stay by me? —

Lucia
[*placidly*]

— The simple truth.

Leo
[*to* Assunta]

Come, my Sister, thou shalt not go away. Nay, if the inn be full, — even so as it was when Our Lady came to Bethlehem, — there shall be some place yet. Think no scorn to rest thee even in a shed, — an if there be a shed . . .

Nicolo
[*with equal beat pointing up under the arch*]

An if there be a shed! — There is a very fine shed indeed; warm as a hay-field and safe as the Duomo. And an ox the finest in Umbria; — he cannot get his horns out of the door without goring any that come down by the steps! Hay? — the finest of any: — take care not to tread it down! And mind you tell the holy Francis this: — I make you free of the shed, free as air of the shed; so long as you tread not down the hay.

The Dyer's Wife

There now, and it *is* a snug place too, tho' Nicolo says it.

The Dyer

As for his donkey, —

The Furrier

—'*Pantaleone!*'

Nicolo

—What of him? What of him?

The Dyer

He is the most marvellous donkey that walks without wings!

Nicolo

So he is! So he is!

The Dyer's Wife

Eh? He cockers and coddles his great ox more than we do our chickens.

Nicolo

—Or your children either,—your children either, since you can't even keep them in a pen!— [*To his daughter.*] Run along with you; fetch the water and have done. I thought it had been the nobleman of France himself, when I looked out and saw the lord bishop's ass.

[*Exit above.* — Brother Leo *assists Assunta to rise from the edge of the fountain; and the gossips ply her with questions to which she seems deaf.*

THE BAKER
[*calling*]

— And why, I ask you, did your man leave you there?

THE DYER

— And why did you try to walk the longest way round to Arezzo?

THE POTTER

— And why did you set down the babe in the snow?

BIMBO *and* BIMBA

Under a juniper-bush she laid it —
— When she saw the robber coming —

JUNIPER

For she mistrusted his benignity. She doubted by the look of his face, how the oil of goodness was wanting in him; — which was indeed true.

BIMBO

— And her man was gathering faggots, just like us —

BIMBA

— When the other caught him. — And it might have been us! —

THE DYER'S WIFE

'T is so, — 't is so, well it might. Oh, heavenly mercy! Be off, little plagues. The worry you cost your granddam this day. You might have been stolen [*cuffing* BIMBO], you might have been lost [*cuffing* BIMBA]. You might have been frozen to the bone; you might have been eaten of wolves, into collops!—[*Cuffing both before her.*] Into the house, little desolations of my life!

LEO
[*to* ASSUNTA]

Come, Lady: and be cheered concerning the babe. For thou shalt rest and think on him who lay, even as thou shalt, among the gentle beasts and warm in the hay.

> [*He takes* ASSUNTA *to the ox-shed under the archway and returns.* BROTHER JUNIPER *collects the faggots up near the foot of the steps and stands forth, rubbing his hands.*

JUNIPER

And where shall the pot be found, for so great a feast? The pot that shall do honor to this vigil, with an abounding *minestrone*—a very lordly noble broth?

The Dyer's Wife

If the pot were all you wanted, holy father, we have a great kettle within,—and empty enough to please you!

> [Bimbo *and* Bimba *fetch out a great iron pot which they take to* Juniper, *with sundry trappings to set it up.*

Bimba

But, Brother Juniper, where is the feast?

Juniper

Why, little pigeons, behold the firewood ready,—and this goodly great pot yawning empty; and here be all the open mouths. It doth but remain for the Lord to send us some little portion of His largess,—that ye may all eat abundantly and be filled!

The People
[*with mixed emotions*]

Ah, ah!

Juniper

Nay, here a little, there a little. We shall put all together and make a great feast, doubt not. Give each the little he hath, — with the little more from up there [*pointing to the upper square*], and it shall be multiplied to all your hungers. —

The People
[*ruefully*]

Ah!

[*The singing of* St. Francis *is heard dimly approaching.*

Juniper
[*wistfully*]

I speak as a fool . . . Yet love bloweth the fire, and the fire shall boil the pot, and — [*the singing nearer.*] Peace, sweet brothers, he comes at last! —

[*Runs up to look under the archway, and calls back.*

He comes, — Brother Francis! — and a most marvellous great dog, leaping beside, — rejoicing with holy gladness!

[*Enter* St. Francis *and* The Wolf]

[For the following scene, THE WOLF prances in, full of buoyancy,—checked every little while by his dread of recognition and by the novelty of the thing. He is filled with curiosity towards place and people.— Now and then he shies violently at a sudden hostile association,— a twinge of conscience—or a scent!

At first he occupies the stage centre, up,— wary and reserved, till FRANCIS beckons him;— rolling his eyes, tongue out, like a sagacious dog.— Later, he dashes in and out of the sheltering arcades, stands on his hind legs and looks in at windows and out on the people. The folk at first show some fear and astonishment; then reassurance, — he seems the dog so completely.

THE PEOPLE OF GUBBIO
[*flocking towards* FRANCIS]

— Blessed Francis! — Blessed Francis! — Francis of Assisi! — Little Poor Man! — Little Poor Man!

JUNIPER
[*all eyes for* THE WOLF]

Brother Francis, little Father! Whoever beheld such a —

The Wolf of Gubbio

BIMBO *and* **BIMBA**

— Oh, what a funny, great big dog!

THE DYER'S WIFE

— Holy Father, what a dog!

THE FURRIER'S WIFE

That hide! Those teeth! —

THE DYER

See, see, see! It's the seraphic little Father's dog! —

LUCREZIA
[*a blind old woman*]

Holy Francis, are you come at last? To keep the feast with us hungry ones? —

THE BAKER

Ay, holy Francis heard us call!

FRANCIS

      Peace be to all!
Peace unto every smallest one
Foregathered here, with Brother Sun.
 [*Touching the children's heads; they draw
  back from* THE WOLF.

The Wolf of Gubbio

Bimba
Oh, Father, what a fearful beast! —
He's so much like —

Lucia
[*with upraised hands*]
— A wolf, at least!

The Women
Ah!

The Dyer
I never saw, — not with these eyes,
A dog of such a size. . . .

The Dyer's Wife
Precisely like a wolf.

The Dyer
— In all ways, like a wolf.
I never saw —

The Baker
Nor I, indeed, —
A dog of such a breed.
Just like a wolf.

OTHERS
    Yes, yes!

FRANCIS
    Indeed,
He *is* so!

THE FURRIER
Girth and hide,—

FRANCIS
[*heartily*]
    And speed!
Sooth, for his name, in case of need,
I call him — '*Brother Wolf.*'
[*They laugh.* — THE WOLF *rolls his eyes as if
words failed.* LEO *and* JUNIPER *approach
him wonderingly.* THE WOLF, *after a
sidelong glance and sniff at each, licks his
hand once; and sits still, lapping his chops
with inexpressible discretion.*

FRANCIS
And for his courtesy? To-day
He fellowed me the livelong way:—
Look, Juniper, he ought to be
A brother of our company;

5 The Wolf of Gubbio

For all his prowess and his pride,
He wears his shirt of hair outside,
. . . Even at the holy tide!

Bimbo
But he's just like a wolf.

Francis
[*heartily*]
       Yea, so!
And do you wish to see him go
Upright, and walking?

Children
       Yes — yes, yes!

Francis
So. Brother, of thy gentleness,
Wilt thou stand up before our sight,
Even as a man, — for more delight,
    And walk upright?

[THE WOLF, *surprised and gratified, tries it and succeeds, to his pride and pleasure. He paces several steps with dignity, and sits down again with a 'Wuff,' — a sneezy note of achievement. Chorus of pleasure from the by-standers.*

The Wolf of Gubbio

FRANCIS
[*to them*]

Ye will have no more fear, to-day?

ALL

— No, no!
— Did you see him walk?
Did you see him play?

[*St. Francis crosses, left, to greet the old people in their doorways. The Wolf, who keeps discreetly near him, examines each interior, standing on his hind legs with quivering interest.*

JUNIPER
[*to* The Baker]

And might it be, dear man, you have a loaf now, or other good thing, to give to the poor soul we found in the woods? And herself laid by to rest in the stable-shed?

THE BAKER
[*querulously*]

Good things? — To give away! Not I, not I. Ah, to be asking good things of me, and for a potter's wife of Foligno, — and my sons away warring at the gate of Perugia!—And not a morsel in the house but what I have to bake with my own hands . . . and scarce a tooth left me . . . and the hard winter on us, and a cold spring coming after . . . and the very Wolf at the door!—

   [THE WOLF *shies suddenly behind the Saint
     with the hint of a growl.*

And the very dogs snarling at the old!—

   [ST. FRANCIS *looks in sweetly, and cheers* THE
     BAKER: THE WOLF *reconnoitres.* THE
     DYER *and his wife greet the Saint by
     their own doorway;—yellow hands on*
     THE DYER, *and blue on his wife.*

       FRANCIS
      [*to* THE BAKER]

Take heart, man dear! this very day
Is bearing blessing on the way.
We little fellows all are here
    To bring you cheer;
That you shall take, and turn, and make
To fair white bread for hunger's sake!

      THE BAKER
                    Eh?

FRANCIS

Gather we all from door to door,
A little, from a little store.
Ah, dear my children, look and see
That little turn a treasury
To certain poorer than ye be!
          [*To* THE DYER'S WIFE]
So, Monna Piera! Come, what cheer?

THE DYER'S WIFE.

— Oh, was there ever such a year!
          [*In one breath*]
Piero gone, Gentile, Giuseppe, all fighting at the gates of Perugia! — Piero's wife ailing, Gentile's wife looking towards another! — Giuseppe had no wife at all to help me with the dye in nowise; — the dye, the children, the chickens! Only myself at the dye-vats with him [*pointing to her husband*] day in, day out. — Like an old hen clucking after three broods at once; — not a moment for a word with a gossip save on the high holy-days; and even then, the color will not off! Look you! [*Holding up her azure hands.*]

[THE WOLF *reënters unnoticed for the moment.*]

80 THE WOLF OF GUBBIO

FRANCIS

Yea, Monna Piera, verily! —
As blue as any fleur-de-lys
The earliest spring can bring to blow
Along a meadow.

THE DYER'S WIFE
[*proudly*]

                    Eh? 'T is so!

THE DYER

—A noble, fast, clinging color, that floods cannot destroy. But who buys? The blue stone I powdered up five years ago is hardly gone; — As for saffron —

THE DYER'S WIFE

—We've never sold enough to pay for the color of his two hands! O Little Man of God, what a year, what a year! 't is all as he said [*pointing to* THE BAKER]; our young men away, and our young women pining, and the hard winter coming, and the Wolf at the door! O Little Poor Man, what a year!

The Wolf
[*aside*]

There's an idea!
[*Exit by* The Dyer's *alley*]

The Dyer

What is the dog growling at?

The Furrier
[*joining them*]

— Why wouldn't any dog growl?— The taxes on fur, Father Francis! I had as lief to keep the live beasts lodging by me, to eat us out of house and home. And now with fighting the Perugians, we shall sell them no fur these twenty years to come. As to this town and lordship, — who buys so much as the ear of a squirrel?

The Dyer's Wife
[*pointing to* The Furrier's Wife]

And who can afford to be wearing a hood set round about with fox-tails?

The Furrier's Wife

To save it from the moths and rust, — the

moths and rust, alone. No one in this desolate sorry spot would spend a soldo on a neighbor's wares.

THE POTTER
[calling out grumblingly]

What is that to me? What is that to me? You can eat up the creatures you catch, and wear their skins after. But if no man buy my pots, can I eat them again? Hee — hee! — I can make little jugs and big jugs, — *scodelle, boccali, tondini!* But I cannot eat them, for all the teeth I have. And they make little jugs and big jugs too, at Foligno, Fossato, Spello, — *Pah!* — And my last son away at the war; — and the harvest a mock, and the vintage worse, and the long winter coming, and the spring after that, and the summer next, but that's not the end; and all with the Wolf at the door! —

> [THE WOLF, *reëntering, shrinks close to* FRANCIS *and paws at him for attention. The children observe it.*

BIMBA

Look, Father, look! Who ever saw —

BIMBO

He has a splinter in his paw!
[THE WOLF *tugs at the habit of* ST. FRANCIS, *with a show of pain. The gossips watch a moment, then resume their wrangling at* THE BAKER'S *doorway; some assist* JUNIPER *to set up his pot with a hook and iron braces.*

THE BAKER

— And well he knows only a holy man would have the patience to take it out of a great wild beast like that. A-ah!   [*With disfavor.*

FRANCIS

Nay, Brother Wolf, come here with me.
Give me thy hand, to see.

THE WOLF

[*muttering rapidly while he submits his paw with some complacency in being petted*]
— Thorn in each paw, and every ear full!
O Little Man, but this is fearful.
. . . . *O miserere!*
How can I be both calm and wary?

How can I look both ways securely?
    — They'll know me, surely.
Hearken. Just now, I made a sally
Into the Dyer's, by that alley.
And there, brimful and just inside,
Is a whole vat, two metres wide,
    A rare, deep blue.
    — Would n't that do? —
No man could ever know this hide;
Come on; — you have me — dyed!
There's saffron there, if you prefer . . .
Not much, though; for it's costlier.
    — Beside,
These cackling wives and make-shift men
Might take me for a sheep-dog then. —

    FRANCIS
    [*laughing over him*]
What, Brother Wolf, for all thy pride,
    And would'st thou hide?

    THE WOLF
    [*nervously*]
Whose hide? — Maybe my courage fails, —
A penance for my sins . . .
But do avoid the man of Skins, —
And his helpmeet, of a hundred tails!

The Wolf of Gubbio

Francis

A kindly man, of wants and woes.
Why should he guess?

The Wolf
[*with scorn*]
— Has he a nose?
[*Walks to leeward of the Saint towards* The Furrier's *empty booth, to view the small exhibit of hanging skins, with fevered curiosity.*
Kind! . . . And what do you think of those? —
[*Sniffs excitedly and shies away, right. The people notice, as* Francis *crosses to them again.*

The Dyer

Eh, eh? No wonder he makes shy of Nello's shop! That skin of his would fetch a fine price any day, — for a mock-wolf hide.

The Wolf
[*overbearing*]
Mock-wolf! Gr—r—r . . .

The Potter
[*from his doorway right*]

Bah! — *via, via!*

[The Wolf *avoids him, and goes to the next door —* Old Lucrezia's *— where he shows signs of panic. She sits in the doorway, blindly spinning, with a little hand distaff.*

The Furrier's Wife
[*complacently*]

Ay, he would make the best of furs.

The Baker

Faith, 't is the crossest of all curs. —

Bimba
[*following* The Wolf]

No, no! — His tail is full of burrs!

The Wolf
[*to himself*]

... Now, will you hear? —

                ... There's an idea!

[*Backs up to* Francis *again, with signs of distress. The people laugh, while* Francis *follows* The Wolf *apart, and inquires of his hurt.*

The Wolf of Gubbio

The Dyer's Wife
Like a great baby! —

Francis
[*to* The Wolf]
 . . . Dost thou ail?

The Wolf
[*in a gruff aside*]
No, no, it's not my tail.
No, it's my past . . . that's on my mind.
Why can't that stay behind?
Hist . . . do you see that woman there?
The old one, with the silver hair?
She'll know me!

Francis
Brother, she is blind.

Bimbo
[*watching from across the way*]
Hear how he whines. —

Bimba
— He had good cause.

BIMBO

— And licks his paws.

THE WOLF
[*while* ST. FRANCIS *strokes his ears, and disengages a burr or two*]

O Little Man, . . . I am not more than human;
— I cannot face that woman.
Look, once . . . Oh, years and years ago, —
Her garden's at the back, you know . . .

FRANCIS
[*with pain and pity*]

Ah, tears of weary women still!

THE WOLF
[*dolorously*]

Say what you will . . .
But is n't it what all wolves do?

FRANCIS

Prey on the helpless? Yea, not you
Alone, my Brother. All wolves do.

The Wolf of Gubbio

The Wolf

And I was hungry . . . after Lent;
    And so . . . I went . . .
  [Whispers to St. Francis, *whose face shows deep feeling.*
Hm-hm. — I did, and open-eyed . . .
  And a young lamb, beside!

Francis

[crossing with sweet concern to Old Lucrezia*]*
  Monna Lucrezia, of your grace,
  Will you sit here, a little space,
  And warm you in the lovely sun,
    Until your weaving's done?
  And this, my Brother here, shall be
  A footstool for you, joyfully;
    To make your comfort full,
    The while you card the wool.
    [She feels her way out into the sunlight, smiling, and sits upon a bench. The Wolf, *obedient to* Francis' *sign, crouches before her, so that she rests her feet on his back. He is the picture of abject misery.*
  And come you, all, till the noon is done,
  Singing and working, every one,
    For praise of Brother Sun!

Shall we not all, both young and old
Sing away want,— sing away cold?
Shall we not make our thresholds sweet,
Even as though we looked to see
Our Lady, riding presently
   Even adown this street?—
[*They catch the infection of his happiness and shed their woes and grumblings suddenly.*

THE BAKER
[*laughing in sudden youth, while they look at him with amazement*]

Eh?— Old as I am, and full of care,—
Yet I could swear,
If holy Francis do but pass,
The snow turns feathers; and all the air
Is mild as Martinmas!
   [*singing*]
I am the Baker of Gubbio;
And the longer I live, the older I grow!
But when I can no more of bread,
Manna shall be my food instead.
   Hosanna,
   Hosanna,
Good wine, and mellow manna!
   [*To* THE POTTER]
Eh? neighbor, are you dumb this day?

The Wolf of Gubbio

Francis

[*to* The Potter, *who is turning a bowl on his wheel*]

Not he, not he! — Whose hands have skill
To turn and shape, and warm at will,
    This cold and trembling clay : —
Of feeble clasp and quivering lips,
    All shaken with dismay;
Ah, *Povero!* the brother-thing, —
A creature weak and perishing, —
Look, through his guiding hand it slips,
Wrought now to stand and laugh, — and sing!

The Potter
[*elated*]
. . . . Eh, eh?
[*He turns his wheel, singing*]
  Ho! Ho! Ho! Ho!
  Round you go, round you go;
  Round as the sun,
    So, — so;
  With a lip to sing,
  And a lip to pour: —
  When the draught is done,
    God send us more!

The Wolf

Bravo! — *wfff* . . .

The Wolf of Gubbio

LUCREZIA
[*singing*]

Weave and spin;
Spin and weave;
Ever since our mother Eve
    Did begin!
Little lamb,—O white of wool,
Keep you white and beautiful.
Give you peace, give you peace;
You shall give me of your fleece.
Never shall Our Lady grieve,
    While I weave,
    While I weave
This,— so moonlike white and fair,
To shield Him from the bitter air,
Her Lamb, her blessed Son,
    . . . Her One.

[*All laugh sweetly in her praise.* THE WOLF *crawls out from under her feet, in dog-like distress of conscience.*

FRANCIS *takes a rush-basket from* THE BAKER'S *window, and turns back to* THE WOLF.

FRANCIS

See, Brother Wolf, I bid thee take

The Wolf of Gubbio

This in thy teeth, a little space;
And even as a helpful hound,
Go now thy round,
Asking of each a little grace,
For pity's sake. —

[*He puts the handle in* The Wolf's *mouth.* The Wolf *trots off with* Brother Leo. *From time to time, he reappears — setting down before* Juniper *various contributions to the pot-au-feu, — a fowl, a string of onions, peppers, a hare.* Juniper *is zealously boiling the pot over the fire, with help and advice from the children, some of whom are mothering small swaddled babies, child-fashion, as they look on.*

Lucia *comes down from the fountain, spilling water out of her copper vessel all the way.* St. Francis *meets her with smiling protest.*

Francis

But . . . of your courtesy, my daughter . . .
Deal gently with her preciousness. —

Lucia

— Eh? —

Francis

.... Yes,—
Our Sister Water.
She is so lowly, and so clear,—
Gladness to see, and mirth to hear;
Laughing, for very purity,
— Laughing to thee and me!

Lucia
[*breaking into song, with other girls who fill their jars also at the fountain*]

Water, water, Sister dear
Silver sweet,— silver clear,
Sweet as laughter in the sun,
Sparkle, drip and run!
Wash the ways before her feet,
Lest there pass along our street,
The blessed, blessed One.

A Caged Blackbird

San Francesco!
San Francesco!
— D'Assisi!
— D'Assisi!
— D'Assisi!

The Wolf of Gubbio

[Juniper *leaves his pot-au-feu, and comes down, pointing out to* St. Francis *the nearest babe, now in* Bimba's *arms.*

Juniper

Seraphic little father, do but see this Babe, how it is marked for the religious life. Poverty and perfect obedience, and silence! Not a word out of him since I came. And his head as bare as a friar's! Heaven itself gave him the tonsure.

Bimba *and* Bimbo
[*laughing*]

Oh, Brother Juniper, it's just a baby. Like any other baby! [*To it.*] Povero! —

[The Wolf, *reëntering at the moment, drops his basket and approaches, to sniff at the centre of interest.*

Bimba

Look! How he loves babies!
[The Wolf *shies off, in sudden panic*]

Juniper
[*of the baby*]

Would he not serve right well, Father Francis, for our vigil and feast this night, of the Crib? — the blessed Babe in the Manger?

ALL
[*excitedly*]

Oh, blessed Francis! — Dear Brother Juniper! Shall we have such a sight? — Here? — Where? — How?

LUCIA

Shall *we* have a show, as the people did at Greccio?

FRANCIS

Sooth, you shall have such blessedness,
You, too, beloved, and no less.

BIMBO *and* BIMBA

With lights?
      — And torches?

LUCIA
      — Banners?

FRANCIS
      Yes!
With all fair things, for loveliness!
Gathered together, every one,
Here in this place when day is done;

And we shall picture, as we may,
The stall where once the Blessed lay,
With ox and ass among the hay.

BIMBA

Oh, lights!

FRANCIS

— Yes, every way of light,
To make the shadow bright; —
To make the dark see clear.
And where is she, — that mothering one
That with her little swaddled son
Shall be Our Lady here?

[LUCIA *would step forward, but* JUNIPER
interposes timidly.

JUNIPER

Father Francis, . . . the poor soul I told you
of, yonder in the ox-shed! — she and the ox-
shed together, put it even in my dull head —

FRANCIS

Yea, so! — and of a certainty,
Right meet it is. This holy night
She shall be crownèd, verily'; —
After her hunger and her thirst,
She that was last shall be the first,
In all men's sight.

LUCIA
[*shrilly*]
— But she's lost the baby!

THE DYER'S WIFE
— And thou hast none!

FRANCIS
And let you take good heed apart,
How you may comfort her sad heart.
As to Our Lady and her Son,
Do honor to this broken one;
Until the wilderness abound;—
And the lost lamb be found.

THE FURRIER'S WIFE
— But which is to be the holy Bambino?

BIMBO *and* BIMBA
— Who is to be for the Baby?

[*The women flock round* ST. FRANCIS, *holding out their swaddled babes for his eyes. The Saint looks on them smiling and touches them tenderly, putting them by, one by one, with a gentle shrewdness.*

THE WOLF OF GUBBIO

FRANCIS

Ah, Monna Piera?

THE DYER'S WIFE
[*proudly*]
. . . Son of my son!

FRANCIS

Sweet peace be on this little one.

LUCIA

Look, look! this *bimba* here, — my niece!

BIMBA
[*calling over its head*]

And mine!

FRANCIS

   The Lord give thee His peace: —
And thee . . . and thee . . . His nested loves!
Sooth, they are like a swarm of doves;
Cooing, and soft . . . and breathing warm,
. . . . . . Doves in a swarm!

THE DYER'S WIFE

Behold him!
[*Thrusting nearer*]

Francis

Ah . . . and yet, methinks .

The Dyer's Wife

Look you, how piously he blinks!

Francis

Yea, so.

The Dyer's Wife

— And warm and rosy-red!

Francis

But ah, my little ones, ye see
When Love the Lord came, verily,
Could He have been so rosy-red,
Who had no shelter to His head?

The Furrier's Wife

Ecco! — 't is liker . . .
[*Holding out her own grandchild*]

Francis

. . . Yet, not quite.
These little hands are folded tight;
And His, methinks, were open wide.

Nothing had He, save love alone,
Who came, a Lamb withouten spot,
Came, in the cold, unto His own:
And they received Him not.
  [*As with a sudden thought*]
Is there, maybe, some smallest one,
Poor of the poorest? — Nay, outcast?
Of all forlorn, the least and last?
Hungering, naked, — turned away
Mayhap this very day? —
Or with no otherwhere to go
Save wandering in the snow?

The Women

No, indeed, little Father! — We be all good mothers here; we give our children the best we have. They never want for anything long, that they want with discretion!

Juniper

[*interposing again with beaming helpfulness*]

Father Francis, the poor woman ye wot of yonder in the ox-shed; that is her case to the last feather! Sore misprized, and turned away, and with no otherwhere to go. —

FRANCIS

Brother, if this be so,
No babe but hers is in such case
To fill that holy place!
Hungering? — Spent, and cold?

JUNIPER
[*enraptured*]
There with the Ox, — behold! —

FRANCIS

An outcast stranger.

THE PEOPLE
[*clamorously*]
— It's lost; it's gone; —
— It's lost! It isn't here!
— It isn't here!

FRANCIS

Still seek it, far and near,
Search every spot.

THE PEOPLE
— Yes, Yes, Yes! —

Francis

And if ye find it not,—

The People

— Yes, yes! — What then?

Francis

Still there will be . . . the Manger!
[*They disperse, trying to conceal their disappointment.*
Reënter at back, Brother Leo *with a basket.*

Leo

These, Brother Francis, my lord the bishop sends to this feast; and would have thee to speak with him shortly, above at the palace.

Juniper

[*opening the basket, and displaying herbs, eggs, and a dressed sucking-pig*]

A most noble . . . little pig . . . of great size [*compassionately*]. Ah . . . brother little Pig! [*faltering.*]

The People
[*delighted*]

In with it,—into the *brodo!* *Evviva* the lord bishop!

Juniper
[*obeying*]

Alas . . . and Alleluia!

Leo

Likewise, my lord the bishop hath given leave to ring the great bell for your assembling, when all is ready.

> [*The Wolf shows some excitement, looking up at the tower.*
>
> *Francis, with a smiling gesture of adieu, makes as if to go; the people disperse to their houses. Brother Leo, up, assists Juniper.*
>
> *The Wolf comes down to meet Francis.*

The Wolf

Lasso! . . . Ah, do not go away;
Some evil thing will chance, I know.
    . . . . Ah, do not go.

Francis

Not yet secure?

The Wolf of Gubbio

The Wolf

No, no. — Ah, stay!
I'm not at ease, not for a minute!
This miming, — why did I begin it?
They'll trap me by the conscience, — and then
    skin it!

Francis
[coaxingly]

Ah! —

The Wolf

They suspect: else why that flick
'Chick nor child, — child nor chick!'
They know the best where things can prick:
— Wf! 'tis a human trick!

*[Dislike and suspicion flare up, in his glances
  towards the houses.*

Francis

Ah no!

The Wolf

But yes! And let me hear once more,
Their endless taunt of *Wolf, Wolf at the
  door!* —

Francis

My Brother! — 'T is no mock at thee.

THE WOLF
[*sternly*]
There is no other Wolf for it to be:
No peer of mine.

FRANCIS
Thou 'rt fevered with remorse.

THE WOLF
[*cautiously*]
N–n . . . Of course.
But I am grown a proverb, do you see?
. . . . . . It 's me.
There is none other like me. No,
I am The Wolf of Gubbio.

FRANCIS
No. 'T is the name they have for poverty.

THE WOLF
[*outraged*]
Their poverty! To put my name
On that black dolor of all shame? —

FRANCIS
The dread of want, that haunts the poor.

THE WOLF
[*barkingly*]
Wolf-at-the-Door? Wolf-at-the-Door?
To blame on *me* their poverty! . . . .
And what of all that went before?
What of their famines and their war
— War — War?

FRANCIS

Even so, Brother. — Come, dost see?
Juniper lacks thy ministry.
He is a true-heart; trust him; — so.

THE WOLF

. . . . . . Ah, must you go?

FRANCIS

To come again.

THE WOLF
[*ruefully*]
. . . . . Ahi! — watch and pray. —
But . . . oh, they'll have my hide some day!
[*Looking back at* THE FURRIER'S]
And if they do, when . . . when I best can
spare it, —

Hist! Poverello, tell me, will you wear it?
None of this folk;—I couldn't bear it!

[*Exit* FRANCIS *with a laughing caress to* THE WOLF'S *ears.* BROTHER LEO *joins him. They go out, centre.* THE WOLF *watches them off, then waddles dejectedly over to* JUNIPER *and the pot, not without suspicion. He utters a whining, experimental note.*]

JUNIPER
[*simply, as to a question*]

Yea, it is so, indeed.
[THE WOLF *shies with astonishment*]

THE WOLF

Wufff.

JUNIPER

Nay, you will like it, I make certain, Brother Wolf; what with rosemary and sweet basil . . .

THE WOLF
[*cautiously*]

Wfff.

Juniper

But only wait till I have cooked all well together, and it will be good . . . better than the raw flesh of Heathenesse. — I crave your pardon, Brother.

The Wolf

What's that? . . .

Juniper

This word I used, of 'Heathenesse.' But you will forgive it, Brother Wolf. For indeed it is very gently done for you to be talking and reasoning with me, — a poor silly simpleton, the fool among the brothers, with no sayings or no words in me at all to match the cunning of the beasts!

> [The Wolf *backs away from him, dumfounded.*

The Wolf

Ha! — . . . Words may fail . . .
                . . . But not a tail. —

> [*Wags it and makes friendly with* Juniper, *who stirs the pot, lifting something to view now and then with his skillet.* . . . The Wolf *on his hind legs looks into the pot.*

JUNIPER
[*stirring*]
Poor Brother Hare!

THE WOLF
[*commiserating*]
Ah, *Povero*,—gone under!

JUNIPER
Would his own mother know him now?

THE WOLF
[*with a flourish of his tongue*]
. . . I wonder.

JUNIPER
Yet, if he needs must perish, to be sure,
He shall as it were—

THE WOLF
Refresh the poor!
Do they go hungry then, another year?
[*Meditates*] . . . Queer.
Bravo, bravo, you're a good fellow.—
Wf!— This broth begins to mellow.
[*Windows open right and left, and inquiring noses turn toward the pot-au-feu.* BIMBO *and* BIMBA *and* THE DYER'S WIFE *appear. She throws a handful of herbs.*

The Wolf of Gubbio

The Dyer's Wife

Brother, Brother Juniper! It will want some spice now . . . I've nothing to throw in the pot, but here's a few herbs!

Children
[*calling*]

Throw them in, and then you'll see!
Basil — fennel — rosemary!

The Potter
[*from his window*]

Yes, and here, some sprigs of bay!

The Wolf

                What are they?
[Juniper *picks them up, and puts them in, while* The Wolf *grins sagaciously at the houses, with growing sarcasm.*
Oh, I see . . . These goodly savors
Call forth unaccustomed favors.
I am not alone there! — No;
Little wolves of Gubbio!   [*Spitefully.*
  [*He crosses and looks in a window*]

WOMAN'S VOICE

Eh? — It's only that wild dog. Be off! — I've nothing more.

THE WOLF
[*aside*]

Nothing? . . . Only when she pleases.
Truly! . . . (Row on row of cheeses.)
Here is somewhat. . . .
[*Missile flies through the window*]

JUNIPER
— *Miserere!*

THE WOLF

Largess, largess!
[*Another follows*]
. . . . . Hm! . . . Be wary . . .
Can't recall that I've abused her. [*Think*
Oh. — But then, . . . an ageing rooster!

JUNIPER
[*stirring*]
. . . . This should be a most exalte
Minestrone.

The Wolf
Is it salted?

Juniper
[*running to a jar*]
Salt, in sooth, more salt. — [*Admiringly.*] Ah, thou!
. . . But if I had some saffron, now, —

The Wolf
Saffron?

Juniper
A pinch.

The Wolf
The yellow in the vat?
— Do you mean that?
[*Goes to the house;* Juniper *marvels*]

Juniper
The Dyer's! San Rufino of Assisi!

The Wolf
. . . . That's easy.
[*Scratches at the door and retreats*]
—You ask him. [The Dyer *looks out.*

THE DYER

If it's anything — Oh, 'tis the wild dog alone.
— Get away!

THE DYER'S WIFE

Be off, then! What do you look for? [*Sees* JUNIPER'S *petitionary attitude.*] Ask the neighbors! As for us, we have n't enough in the cupboard for chick nor child; and the long winter before us, and the bad vintage behind us, and the Wolf— [*The door slams.*
[THE WOLF *shies off, looking ugly*]

JUNIPER

I would that our sister's heart might be warmed of holy Charity, to go comfort her in the ox-shed. — [*Pointing up.*] 'Chick nor child,' —alas!— And where is hers, this winter day?
[THE WOLF *glares at him with sudden suspicion.* JUNIPER *innocently rambles on, stirring.*
How would it wound her to the quick!— Poor soul, withouten child or chick.
[THE WOLF *mutters, still eying him*]
Nay, Brother. Is it lacking aught?
[THE WOLF *shrinks from him, towards* THE BAKER'S *house.*

The Baker
[*thrusting his head out*]

Yah!—Be-off!—Get you gone, *Lupone*,—
Rubaccio! Via—via—via!
[*Throwing an empty flask at him*]

Juniper

'T is done. 'T is done ... smoking and ready;
now will I ring the bell.

The Wolf
[*harshly*]

—And then,
The pack comes scrabbling back again;
The creatures yapping discontent;—
Animals that have lost their scent!
Noble reason throned, indeed!—
To hunt and fight and feed!
[*He begins to look devilish*]

Juniper
[*mildly, his hands folded*]

Ah, Brother Wolf, I would n't say that. For
who can upbraid them, disheartened as they are
with the war and the cold,—

The Wolf

'*And the long winter coming!*'—Yes? Yes? Yes?—*And! and! and!*—

Juniper
[*seriously*]

Yes, and a sorry vintage.—And the very Wolf at the door! [*He turns, not noticing* The Wolf's *fury, and goes up as if to ring the bell: then turns back.*] Stay! First will I sweep all clean . . . Had I a broom now?. . [*Looks doubtfully right and left.*] I will go and ask my lord bishop, in the name of the blessed Michael and all angels, . . . to lend me a broom! Then is there nought left save to ring the great bell.

[*Exit.*

The Wolf
[*alone*]

[*His voice and manner change him to a crackling cynic*]

The Bell. [*He glances upward.*] So this was all it meant. . . . I knew it wouldn't last.—One of these sudden conversions. . . . Voice . . . face . . . music . . . queer feelings . . . —Then where is it all?—I wouldn't be a man if I could. There's only one, [*with a sidelong*

glance after FRANCIS' *exit*] . . . probably not a man at all; something new. — Perhaps back in the woods — Wf! [*Showing sudden abject guilt, as he steals a look at the ox-shed.*] . . . If he knew that? Not he! . . No. [*Defiantly.*] I will have my day, I will have my day! . . . And after, — back to the woods. Ah, where's the use?
. . . .
. . . . . . What was I left watching for?
. . . . . . Saints could do no more!
[*Dashes from house to house, peering in, trying the next window, and muttering with growing excitement.*
Hm! — One rocking at a cradle; —
Baling something with a ladle . . .
Tying kerchiefs; . . . making fine . . .
[*A slap is heard and outcry of children*]
Two — three — four . . . and all to dine?
Ah, my beauty, why such airs? —
Hi! The potter . . . saying his prayers!
Tries her wimple . . . what a wearer!
Just one snarl, now, would it scare her?
(Lento, lento) . . . *Buona sera!*

. . .

Washing, truly. Dozing? Heaven! —
Three, no, no, — four, five, six, seven

Hungry humans ... Call it theft!
Eight? — There will be nothing left.
  [*Goes to* THE FURRIER'S: *stands up, quivering with excitement at sight of the skins, recognizing old friends.*
Hide and hair, it makes me creep! ...
Isn't this worse than taking sheep
When you're hungry? — Steal and wear
Others' skins? to make you fair?
Murderers so debonair!
Ah, ah! —   [*With an outburst of grief.*
            So this was where she went,
For all the longing search we spent! ...
Oh, Silver Glory's radiant fur!
What woman lives to match with her?
Wind-swift! — Her eyes two yellow suns! —
Fighting for all her little ones,
The cursèd winter Snarl was trapped ...
— If ever I see a woman wrapped
In all that beauty not her own,
That strength she could not meet alone, —
Something she never fought nor fed,
Cold — stolen — duped and dead! —
  [THE FURRIER'S *wife, speaking back, appears at the window, takes down a mantle of wolf-skin and puts it over her shoulders, complacently.*

The Wolf of Gubbio

The Furrier's Wife

— And *I* say I will! For the dusk will be falling cold. And this nobleman of France may be there to look on ... and what is it worth outside, but to gather dust and covetous desires?

[*Exit within.*

The Wolf
[*savagely*]

Never again shall *my* guilt vex my wits.
. . . . . . We're quits!

[*With a snarl, he runs up to the pot, and tramples out the fire beneath. — He stands upright and plunging nose and paws into the pot, voraciously devours everything.*

From the pot he crosses to the fountain and loudly drinks his fill; pausing to grin with spite, back at the little houses, flourishing his tongue. Shying away from the ox-shed, which he always avoids, he goes up the stone steps on all fours, and disappears, right.

Enter, up left, on the steps, Louis of France, *followed by his men. All wear pilgrim robes, with palmers' emblems upon them. He descends the steps, and speaks back to them, pointing out the smoking kettle, smilingly.*

LOUIS

Pause here. Ye see? The feast is ready set.
To-day shall we break bread with God's own
  poor;
And with the holy Francis.
> [*Enter below, under the archway,* JUNIPER
> *beaming with joy,— a twig-broom in his
> hand, and a white linen cloth on his arm.*
> JUNIPER, *not noticing* LOUIS, *brushes off
> the flag-stones round about the kettles first.
> Then, seeing the strangers, he advances,
> with timid hospitality.*

JUNIPER

The Lord give ye His Peace. —

LOUIS

      And thee, my brother.
Wilt thou admit a pilgrim?

JUNIPER

Ah, Messer Pilgrim, God's guests are everywhere. — Now am I about to ring the great
bell . . . Then comes little Father Francis
. . . then all! —
> [*He hastens up and rings. The people come
> in with great expectation as the Bell sounds.*

Enter Francis *and* Brother Leo — *who meet* Louis, *without knowing him, but with radiant friendliness.*

Juniper *returns and hastens to the pot. Plunging in his ladle, he is seen to discover with consternation that it is empty; and stands, first incredulous, then rooted to the ground with woe.*

Francis

Peace be upon you! . . . and on all
This homing flock . . .
        [*To* Louis]
    My Brother dear!
        [*To* Juniper]
Nay, Juniper . . . But what mischance
Doth cloud thy countenance?

Juniper
[*gaspingly*]
Seraphic little . . . I . . .
      . . there's no . . .
              . . . 't is clear
An Angel hath been here . . .
. . . .
    The pot is . . . empty! —

The People of Gubbio

My gander . . . my gander . . . the best of them all! — The pot is empty . . . the pot is empty! No festa, no dinner, no *minestrone!* — Oh! Oh! my peppers, my peppers . . . the two last eggs! Gone! — Gone! Devoured! Devoured! Devoured!

The Furrier's Wife *and* The Dyer's Wife

An angel indeed! Hear the simple brother who knows not the ways of angels from the ways of ravening beasts! Thieves, thieves it was! —

The Baker *and* The Furrier

'T was that wolfish cur, — that Beelzebub of a dog, that watched by the pot when last we saw him. — No, no! He couldn't — He wouldn't — No, no! You lie!

The Children
[*weeping*]

Oh, oh! The pig! — The little pig — the pretty little pig from the palace!

FRANCIS
[*soothing them*]
Children, all shall yet be well:
... Trust the blessed spell
Or this Vigil that we keep.
Nay, beloved, do not weep.
Mayhap, for pity of your case,—
Friend Nicolo will do you grace,
... After a little space.

[NICOLO, *on the street steps, raises his hands in horror. Unable to argue with* FRANCIS, *he begins to count beads, with increasing desperation.*

FRANCIS
[*to the strangers smilingly*]
And pardon, gentle Pilgrims all,
Our emptiness, our windy hall.
Yea, though ye be full travel-worn
    Yet ye will think no scorn.
And though ye hunger verily,
    Pray you, bear with me.
Since neighbor Nicolo, indeed
    Hath his right need

To make all ready,—to prepare
For guests so many ... unaware;—

[NICOLO's *despair bursts out afresh*]

Holiday hungers, many more
Than he had reckoned for!

[FRANCIS *takes the white cloth from* JUNIPER *who still stands motionless, and with the playful deliberation of a child, spreads it on the ground in the centre, while all watch open-mouthed, charmed into attention,—a quiet circle.*
Right, behind the by-standers, reappears THE WOLF, *rolling his eyes as if he defied the situation, till the voice of* FRANCIS *makes him also a listener, lost to all else. No one sees him. When the folk sit down, at* FRANCIS' *bidding, he starts up with a dog's excitement at the matter in hand, showing his surprise and curiosity; coming down, by degrees, nearer those who sit with their backs turned towards him. Pangs of conscience alternate with his interest, and wistful looks towards* FRANCIS.

FRANCIS

See. I spread this fair white cloth
For our table. . . . Be not wroth.

[Coaxingly]

Cheer thee, Juniper, my brother!
May we not pledge one another
Circled, brother-wise, around?—
. . . Here upon the ground?

[He sits: they follow suit]

See. Our court is acres wide;
Guests flock in from every side;
Let us, even as Love would,
Share the bread of brotherhood.

LOUIS
[to FRANCIS]

Savors of immortal cheer
Fill us all that listen here,
  Holy man and dear.

FRANCIS

Nay, sweet brother: naught I can
Save as a little, base poor man!

But you, of your fair courtesy
Shall fill us all with warmth and glee;
Yea, as it were with minstrelsy!
[*The people are quickened;* The Wolf *comes down, listening, behind the right-hand corner-group.* Francis *turns eagerly to* Louis *and his companions.*
As, at the feast, the minstrel chants
High deeds of knighthood and of war,
Of Charles the Emperor, and sweet France,
Ballad and gest and blithe romance, —
Be ye our troubadours!
Tell us poor stay-at-homes that be,
Of Saracens beyond the sea, —
Desert and palm, and holy shrine;
Of Acre, and of Palestine!
Yea, — all that won for thee this sign.
[*He leans across to* Louis, *to look at the crusader's emblem upon the king's habit.* Louis *unfastens it and leans towards him to show it.* — *The other knights do likewise with theirs, and the villagers cluster close.* Louis *is clearly seen in profile, left,* Francis *facing the spectators, in the centre of the group.*
Enter, down left, — *round the corner-wall of* The Furrier's *house, the two thieves,*

Grillo *and* Vecchio Vecchio, *unnoticed by the crowd.*
They look upon this gathering with open-mouthed surprise, soon spying Louis.

Grillo
[*hoarsely*]

It's himself, in spite of all; — the man of France. Mark you that nose?

Vecchio Vecchio

What game are they at? . . . They've borne off the food.

Grillo
[*still staring*]

It's his nose.

Vecchio Vecchio

And what good is his nose to me? Do you see the miniver up his sleeve?

Grillo

That nose . . . I saw it on horseback . . . I can't miss it afoot. Look ! . . .
[*They whisper*]
[The Wolf, *to the right, sniffs warily high in air, then looks about for the cause of his unrest.*

THE WOLF
[*apart*]
That scent? . . . It can't be . . . *Wf!*
[*He follows his scent, left, and perceives* Grillo *and* Vecchio Vecchio. *At the same moment they see him.*

Vecchio Vecchio
Death of my life! —

Grillo
No, no, —

The Wolf
[*ominously*]
Gr-r-r-r . . . .
[*People turn to look at* Grillo *and* Vecchio Vecchio, *who are struggling to join the circle for protection.*

Vecchio Vecchio *and* Grillo
Gentlemen, lords — . . . No — no matter,
—— We are . . . we are very fond of dogs!
—— I like dogs . . . Dogs like me.

THE WOLF
[*ferociously*]

Sguarda! . . . .

GRILLO

The Wolf of Gubbio!

[*They rush out, mad with fright. — General uproar. — The villagers spring up and shout, huddled together.* — Louis *rises and his men stand by him.*

Francis *lifts his hand for quiet, and crosses to* The Wolf.*

WOMEN
[*screaming*]

Father, it's the devil himself — Seeking to undo you! —

Ah, *Lupone, Rubaccio!* — Beast! Beast!

MEN

Kill him — kill him — kill him! No, it's a dog — No, it's a Wolf — A dog — a Wolf — the Wolf of Gubbio, — the Wolf of Gubbio!

FRANCIS

Peace!

All the People

'Twas he emptied the pot! — He stole the broth. — I saw him — I heard him — I knew it. The simple brother left him alone with the pot. 'Twas he ate up our feast of a year! 'Twas he ate our chickens and sheep these years gone by! — No, no, it's a dog! — The devil's own dog! —

— Look you! How ashamed he is already! Even as a dog he is telling you, — he did it!

[THE WOLF *goes abjectly prostrate at the feet of* FRANCIS. — *The people pick up stones.*

Francis

Hush. Little children, will you grieve
The heart of God? — This eve?
Your brother has confessed.
. . . . He is your guest.
Heavy indeed his debt to you, and sore.
— Forgive the more.
[*Murmurs*]
There is no need to tell: you know.
This is . . . the Wolf of Gubbio.
[*Renewed rage and fear*]

And all these years, and all these years,
He wrought you havoc, hunger, tears;
He filled the dark with fears.
Yet this one day,—from his safe wood,
He came to crave your brotherhood,
    If ye but understood.
The dog that served so faithfully
This hour gone by, was none but he.
. . . I was the sinner,—I,
    To leave him lone——

ALL

            No, . . . he must die!
He must die!—With a stake through his heart!
—Kill—kill—kill him!

FRANCIS

Hark! . . . Know you not, on this high feast,
There is a truce, 'twixt man and beast?
    —Ye may not touch the least
Of brother creatures vengefully;—
Nor hurt, nor hound him that he die. —
That pact between you, ye shall keep:
Unless you will Lord Christ to weep,
  . . . . Even Lord Love, on high!

My little wolves . . . fear not! Let cease
Your anger, save it be with me.
And Brother Wolf shall go in peace.
> [*Murmurs die out, and spring up. The people are backing away fearfully, when* The Dyer's Wife *stumbles against one of the French knights and screams.*]

The Dyer's Wife

Ah, ah! . . . Look there, too! If he have
not a sword under the robe of a holy palmer!
What pilgrims are these! What holiday for
poor folks! —

Louis

> [*to* Francis, *reassuring all*]

Yea, brother, think no ill; — 'tis no disguise.
Only of wont, my men are armed with swords,
To do you service; seeing we are indeed
All fellow-pilgrims . . . from the Holy Land.
And I . . .
> [*He hesitates, then says with meaning*]

. . . thy Brother Louis . . . Louis of France.

People

— Eh, it is a great lord then, . . . —
A mighty baron —! —

Francis
[*not knowing him, but with simplest blithe courtesy*]

And welcome, Brother Louis, from sweet France!

Louis

Happily come... to beg all ye, good friends,
[*To the people*]
Be guests of mine; and suffer me, me too,
To bear a candle at your festival.

Juniper
[*approaching timidly*]
My lord Sir Pilgrim...

Louis

      Brother Juniper?
Tell me, what can I, or these gentlemen
To speed the holy feast?

Juniper
[*in a breathless outburst*]

Ah, lords and barons, and Sir Brother Knight! Your gentlemen, there it is!— If they might but search the woods now,— before sundown; nay, 't is well-nigh on us . . . but with torches! Sure, any lost soul would follow a torch! — And if they could but find and bring and save, the good man, and the lost babe, of this poor soul yonder in the ox-shed! . . . She that is to figure to us this night, Madonna Queen of Heaven, with that crib, and that hay, and the ox, and the ass, and the manger! — For except we find and bring her man to be Holy Joseph, and her babe to be a babe indeed, — the Blessed Babe, — there will be nothing left us for a spectacle, but a sorry, rueful, out-of-measure poor little fragment of a Holy Family!

Louis
[*warmly*]

Blest be thy heart, my Brother. We'll make search!

Francis

Take comfort, Juniper.

Children
To-night! —

                    To-night!

Francis

  — With every man his light!
[*They all withdraw, taking the longest way round from* The Wolf, *with reviving sullen murmurs.* Francis *points to* The Wolf, *solemnly.*
And keep the pact of his release.
   [*To* The Wolf]
.... My Brother, go in peace.
[*They go into their houses and bar the doors. Exeunt* Louis *and his men by the steps.* Leo *and* Juniper *up, wait for* Francis, *who lingers beside* The Wolf.
The Furrier's Wife *calls from her window shrilly.*

The Furrier's Wife

Father, a wolf's a wolf! — Don't trust him. A beast is n't a man, and never will be. A wolf will never put on human ways! — No, never, never!

Francis
[*smiling*]
    Ah, ... but yes
— When men put off their wolfishness.

[The light wanes; with the quickness of sunset in a mountain place.—There is a sound of bolts drawn and doors barred. The Wolf *is still silent and prostrate.*

Francis

Brother, and is thy hurt so sore?

The Wolf
[muttering]

'Wolf-at-the-door' . . .

Francis

Nay, go in peace. And comfort thee;
. . . Behold, thou 'rt free.
[He points up, and with a slow caress on The Wolf's *head, he goes out under the archway with* Leo *and* Juniper. The Wolf *gets up from the ground and looks miserably, with hanging head, at the shut houses, right and left; then shambles heavily up the square, pausing midway.*

The Wolf

Yet have I not deserved to be
Their by-word name for Misery.
Men cast their wolfishness on me!

[*Snarlingly*]
Big wolves and little, — hutch and hall,
Raven upon each other, all : —
Each on the lesser, — day by day,
They snatch and cheat and rend their prey;
Warring together, great and small ; —
. . . Yes, warring all ! —
The very bread they struggled for,
They spill and waste in war — war
. . . . War! . .

[*Going up, and with his paws on the steps,
  he turns to look back on the square.*
That day, when I would gather more
Of ravening greed, and wolfish lore,
I will seek out the homes of Men;
I will seek out their feasts again. —
Let them cry aloud, and call me, then,
  '*Wolf-at-the-Door* . . .
      Wolf-at-the-Door!
. . . . . *Wolf-at-the-Door!*'

Curtain.

*The Little Poor Man touched my heart;
With love, with love, it broke.
And from my bonden death-in-life,—
I woke.*

Act III

Scene: *The same square at dusk. Above the arch, the glimpse of sky glows peacock-blue; with the Evening Star.*

The archway is now filled in with a hanging composed of various stuffs and garments,— deep green, blue and olive, fastened together to make a curtain. At the left-hand edge of this home-made curtain, a crack of light gleams upon a string of children, one behind another who are peering in.— The only other light comes from the faintly glimmering shrine, in the corner-wall, which makes a tiny lunette of dim color.

Down to the right, by The Potter's *bench,* The Wolf *watches, motionless and miserable.*

Bimba, *giving place to another child for a moment at the peep-hole, turns about dancingly, singing.*

Bimba

STAR, Star!
　　Star, Star! . . . . .

OTHER CHILDREN
[*singing in little high voices*]
Star, Star!
Star, Star!

BIMBA
[*peeping in*]
Look, look! Who'd ever guess it was the woman of Foligno? She looks all shining, like Our Lady.
[*They press together, to see*]

BIMBO
But she's been weeping, too; you can see.

BIMBA
You can see her tears ... shining in the torchlight.

CHILDREN
[*singing*]
Star, Star,
Star, Star!
Star, Star! .....
[*The sound of a song in the distance attracts their attention for an instant.*

The Wolf of Gubbio

MEN'S VOICES
[*without*]

The Lord of highest Heaven,
Fair Lord Emmanuel,
Shall come at last, this even,
With famished men to dwell!
My heart, be as a bell,
 Noël, Noël!
And call unto the calling stars,
'All's well! All's well!'
 Noël, Noël, Noël!

THE WOLF
[*wretchedly, to himself*]

The world goes by,
The world goes by;
The stars smile down,
And then pass by.
[*Looking up*]
The great Star shines, and will not see.
The small stars prick me with their scorn.
Each look is sharper than a thorn . . .
Love is for every soul but me.

BIMBO

[*peering behind the archway curtain*]

Look at the Ox, . . . Nicolo's Ox! . . . They are going to lead him out . . . Oh! . Oh!

BIMBA

Now she cannot weep any more.

BIMBO

His horns are as wide as the moon!

BIMBA

Wider than the moon: . . . wider than the moon! And his eyes are as big as the doorway; and his coat is as white as the snow! Oh, Nicolo's Ox was never so beautiful before, — never, never so beautiful!

THE WOLF

The Ox!

> [*With unquenchable curiosity he creeps nearer, lagging with jealous pain. He goes into* THE POTTER'S *empty house, and tries the window, comes out restlessly, goes to* LUCREZIA'S *house, and thrusts the door open, coming out to listen to the sing-song of the* CHILDREN.

Bimbo

She ought to be content now, with everybody treating her like the Queen of Heaven.

Bimba

But it's only for to-night. To-morrow she'll be just like anybody else, and as if it were last Monday; . and it's not back to Heaven she will be going, but only to Foligno. . . . Besides, you see, she wants her baby, — her own one!

[THE WOLF *drops his nose wretchedly, takes his paws from the sill, and shambles out with increasing dog-like anguish. He squeezes behind the stone bench along the house, and rests his nose on top of it, still watching. The Song approaches, — sung by the King's men, off.*

Men's Voices

The stars that be God's liegemen
Along His towers on high,
They lift aloft their torches
To light the dark hosts by.
Men, each and all, let cry,
    Noël, Noël!

Call to the stars above our wars,
'All's well! All's well!'
Noël, Noël, Noël!
[BIMBO *scampers up the steps after the sound*]

BIMBA

It's the French knights, coming from the mountain! — They've found him, — they've found him, — they've found her man!
[*Reënter* BIMBO, *from above*]

BIMBO

The man, the man, the man, they've found him! They've bound him up, they've put a fine coat on him! . . . He's coming to be Holy Joseph, — standing by the Manger.

CHILDREN
[*ecstatically*]

Holy Joseph, standing by the Manger!
[*The tent-curtains part, and* ASSUNTA *is seen to look out with agonized hope. Enter, above, three men with torches, conducting* GIUSEPPE, *a dark and comely peasant, wrapped in a borrowed cloak, with his arm in a sling.* ASSUNTA *steps out, letting the curtain fall, and stretches out her arms.*

The Wolf of Gubbio

GIUSEPPE

Assunta, Assunta! —

ASSUNTA

. . . . The Bambino?
[*They reach their arms to each other, each seeing that the other has it not.*

GIUSEPPE

Ah!
[*They embrace each other, in stricken silence*]

ASSUNTA
[*pointing in*]

One there . . . has hope . . .

GIUSEPPE

Hope? . . . Ah . . .

ASSUNTA

. . . The Poverello!
[*They go in despairingly.* THE WOLF *cowers and listens.*

BIMBA
[*to* BIMBO, *coming down*]

Oh . . . do you . . . suppose . . . ?

BIMBO
[*defiantly*]

Nobody knows.

Bimba

[*weeping*]

But . . . if we'd never run away,
. . . . . . To-day . . ?
She called, — she did, . . . to tell us where
   it lay!

Bimbo

[*sulkily*]

And if six men can't find it, how could we find it? We might have been stolen ourselves.

Bimba

Oh! Oh! . . . What if the Wolf —

Bimbo

[*stoutly*]

He wouldn't dare! — Would he ever put his nose in Gubbio after that? Wouldn't he be a dead Wolf now, if holy Francis hadn't made us promise? . . . Who'd keep it after that? Come back . . . let's see what they're doing now. — It's all dark here.

Bimba

Every candle up above . . . going round the Duomo. — All the people, — all the can-

dles, going along like little stars in the dark.
. . . And Grandmother made a great wax-
light; and she's going to let me hold it. Only
it must keep from now till the feast of the
three Kings! . . . Oh!

> [*Discerning* THE WOLF's *head, and backing
> up, fearfully,* BIMBO *after her.*

Oh, come, come — quick! — Stay close to
holy Francis!

BIMBO

He . . . he's asleep!

> [*They scurry back to the curtain and the ab-
> sorbed group, left.*

THE WOLF

I to live on, alone, apart,
Warming this pain in my old heart!
Still with the snows that melt and drip,
Gnawing my paws for fellowship!
Looking, far, on the lights below;
Little house-lights of Gubbio!
Deh! . . . Lasso! . . . . Wff. . . .

> [*The curtain parts slightly, and* FRANCIS
> *steps out towards* THE WOLF, *who goes
> haltingly to meet him.*

The Wolf of Gubbio

Francis

Brother, and didst thou call? —

The Wolf
[*huskily*]

Yea, so.
How should you know? . . .
I only wait one human sign,
After this life-long, aching fast
Of silence; one more word of thine! —
The last.

Francis

The last?

The Wolf

One word, one man-word spoken,
Before the midnight breaks your spell,
And God takes back His miracle, . . .
And truce is broken!

Francis

Ah, Brother, this shall never be! —
That any love 'twixt thee and me
Be shattered. That were misery.

THE WOLF
[*suffering*]

Oh, if you knew, ...
You, too!
And what care I? —
Liefer I am at once to die,
Than feel slow fires of tortured pride;
Seeing Love is; — but I must bide
Forevermore outside!

[JUNIPER *enters hurriedly from behind the curtain*]

JUNIPER

Brother Francis, — Brother Francis, — the people will be coming now. Once around the Duomo they are going! [*Pointing above.*] And oh, Brother Francis, they will see a miracle this night; — they will hear praise from the Ox and the Ass! For the Ass is taking thought, with his eyes fixed on the torches; and the breath of the Ox goes up like incense, marvellous warm and white on the cold of the air! Let us watch for the miracle!

> [FRANCIS *goes up, beckoning* THE WOLF *to stay. The* CHILDREN *cluster round* JUNIPER *and the curtain.* THE WOLF *withdraws slowly down.*

CHILDREN

O Brother Juniper, O Brother Juniper!

BIMBA

Will he speak this night? Will the Ox speak? — So that we all can hear?

JUNIPER

Why not, little fledglings, why not? Since the Holy Night is drawing on; and only now he moved his great eyes towards me; and I heard with my heart as it were the sound of a bell! Have faith! Have patience. —

CHILDREN

What will the Ox say?

JUNIPER

Why, he will praise the Lord, surely. But whether with Hosanna or Our Father, I cannot tell.

[*Bell sounds from the Duomo*]

CHILDREN

Oh! Oh!

[*Some scamper up the steps to join the procession above. A few remain with their noses at the crack of light.*

THE WOLF

[*looking up towards the bell*]

Yea, and I hear! Oh, rarely well
You wove the spell ...
Beckoning voice far-off, ... Bell!
  [*The bell sounds*]
Warm, and softly, you led below,
Here, to the men of Gubbio!—
Out of that lone and listening wood,
Dreaming a dream of brotherhood!—
  [*Bitterly*]
Hush;—wait; you shall sound my knell.
Only a little!—I come again.—
Only a few sands more, and then ...
  [*Bell*]
Farewell!   [*He runs out, wildly, right.*
[*Enter down, also from the right, the two thieves,* VECCHIO VECCHIO *and* GRILLO, *puzzled at the changed aspect of the square, by reason of the blocked archway.*

VECCHIO VECCHIO

What's towards, now? This is the maddest lunatic town I ever fell on!—

Grillo

Will you see that? Where is the gateway gone? Were we not here? Or have we rounded on ourselves?

Vecchio Vecchio

Per Bacco! Thou 'rt besotted. This is the place; the very place where we sat waiting for them to set on the food. Look you, the same. The archway there is blocked with some holiday show.

Grillo

An ever I am able to tell east from west again, — or right from left, or a wolf from a man! We were fools to take to our heels. But when I saw the old devil there, rearing and bristling, even as this morning on the mountain . . . [*Shivers.*] . . . I see wolves everywhere!

Vecchio Vecchio
[*laughing feebly*]

Thou 'lt be telling it was a Wolf we passed now in the dark . . . running possesst through the brambles, — in too much haste to eat us! . . . But if it had been the Wolf indeed, —

he were slain and skinned by this, and his ears nailed up on the gate —!
[*They inspect the house fronts*]

Grillo
[*rallying*]

Thou 'rt right, Old Cheese! 'T is the place, and the arch, and the lower square, of the lordly city of Gubbio. — [*Pointing.*] Duomo; — fountain; — tanner's, — by the breath of this byway!

Vecchio Vecchio
[*pointing*]

And by this master show . . . What if . . .
[*Approaching* The Furrier's]

Grillo

No, no, show me first what 's back of yon gallimaufry curtain. Show me first where lies the man of France!
[*They tiptoe towards the curtain*]

Vecchio Vecchio

Oho! And this is the day when friars feast. Wine flowing freely; and some noble show set forth, not without noble gazers, unannounced.

156 THE WOLF OF GUBBIO

[*Speaking back to* GRILLO]
'Follow me on!' . . . Then, lordings, by your leaves, ...
— An if it please you . . . .
   [*Enter from the archway,* FRANCIS, *his eyes
   full, smiling on the two, without surprise.*

FRANCIS

Welcome, . . . Brother Thieves!
   [*They stand rooted to the earth, — robbed
   of their breath, — like creatures at bay.*
   FRANCIS *lets the curtain fall behind him,
   and steps out into the dusk towards them,
   encouragingly, shading his eyes a moment,
   the better to see. He speaks with friend-
   liest cheer.*
Nay, beseech you, do not go.
So the torch-light dazzled me,
. . . Hardly might I know.
Yea, but now, in verity,
Seeing it is none but ye,
Brothers, of your courtesy,
Do not go.
I will not, Brothers, that ye be
Such castaways of misery, —
And your lives in jeopardy,

. . . Men under ban :—
Nay, but each one a joyful man.
Come in, come hither, and in God's name,
Suffer ye now no blame.
[*Their faces are convulsed with doubt, amazement, irony.*
But take your comfort, and draw near,
. . . Without hurt or fear.
Warm your hearts against this sight !—
Since our Lord is host to-night.
— I will be your warranty,
Men shall do you right.
[*They come down slowly as if they were unable to walk.* FRANCIS *goes up the steps to meet the procession.*

GRILLO
[*wanly trying to chuckle*]
' Such misery ! '
[*His face is twisted with want.*

VECCHIO VECCHIO
[*dully*]
' Hurt or fear ! ' But it was he . . .

GRILLO

It was he . . . the same. It was he of the woods this morning . . . a little thin fellow.

[*Twitching his fingers as if he remembered his clutch of* ST. FRANCIS' *shoulder.*

. . . I am stark madman now, I know.

VECCHIO VECCHIO
[*as the voices approach*]

We durst not stay. . . .

GRILLO

. . . . We durst not go!

[*The procession comes down the steps led by two Pifferari; the French knights singing, with* LOUIS; *then the women; then the men; all with candles;* FRANCIS *and* FRA LEO *falling in last.* GRILLO *and* VECCHIO VECCHIO *withdraw, down to the left, clearly not daring to run away; and watch all that happens, surprised into open-mouthed subjection.*

THE KNIGHTS

Now fair lord Gabriel speed us
Who march not forth to war;

But seeking out that little Child
And following on the Star!
All we His liegemen are; —
    Noël, Noël! —
Both shepherd-folk and men of might,
And kings that come from far!
    Noël, Noël, Noël!

[*As they range themselves by the upper arcades expectantly, right and left,* FRANCIS *stands forth before the curtain.*

FRANCIS

Welcome, beloved! Welcome ye
All met in one glad company;
Each one a singing and a light
To praise the holy night! —
Like little sorry stars we are,
And dim and small and late and far,
That follow the one Star.
But yet one treasure do we bring,
As liegeman to their king: —
Love, love, down-showered, — and love
    outpoured
Over the world, on every thing,
From Love that is sole lord.

[With the radiance of a child]
O heart! thou little rueful cup,
Fill thee brimful; be lifted up!
O heart, — thou little cup of earth,
What should be likened to thy mirth
Or to the radiancy thereof,
    So thou wert filled with Love?
No heart so dark nor so forlorn
That, if it were fulfilled of Love,
The star that most exults above,
Could laugh his gift to scorn.
But then indeed the stars shall sing
With men, for glory of one thing: —
When that True Love is born.

CHILDREN
Star, Star,
Star, Star! . . .

FRANCIS
Ah, dearest ones, there is one word to tell.
Where Love is not, can be no miracle: —
Where Love is, . . . All is well!

THE PEOPLE
Noël, Noël!

FRANCIS
[*at the curtain*]
Now, Love Himself shall be our Host;
And not in castle nor in hall,
But yonder, in a stall . . .
Even as an outcast stranger,
Fain to be homeless with the uttermost.
Behold, . . . the Manger!

[Leo *and* Juniper *draw back the curtains. Torch-light turns the archway to a golden lunette, with its Holy Family.* Assunta *robed as the Virgin leans above an empty manger;* Giuseppe, *grave and comely, as* St. Joseph, *with a crook;— at back the great white Ox, behind a bin of hay, and the Ass beside. The background is filled with hangings and greenery. The people are struck with awe and delight.*

GRILLO
[*down to* Vecchio Vecchio]
Are we living or dead?

VECCHIO VECCHIO
If we be dead, then this is Judgment.

GRILLO
[*in a whisper*]

Nay, it is the town of Gubbio . . . and the man yon, . . . is the man . . . on the cliff . . .

VECCHIO VECCHIO

And . . . . She is . . .

GRILLO

The woman of Foligno. . . .

[*At the close of the Noël above, THE WOLF has reappeared down by THE POTTER'S wall, breathless, burrs and brambles in his coat and ears. He looks and retreats; reappears in the open doorway of OLD LUCREZIA's house, and watches there awhile. He is panting, and evidently in extremity of wretchedness. No one sees him; all are rapt in the welcome of ST. FRANCIS. BIMBO and BIMBA explain all to OLD LUCREZIA, who listens with beatific pleasure.*]

BIMBA

—And Blessed Mary the Virgin,—and Holy Joseph, and the Manger!

Bimbo
— And Joseph has a crook.

Bimba
— And Mary has a veil. And the Ox and the Ass are there!

Bimbo
And torches, — lights in every place!

Lucrezia
I feel them shining . . . on my face.

Francis
Come then, beloved, and draw near;
Let us make offering here.
For we, that be not great nor wise,
Shall we not gladden our poor eyes,
Even to the last and least,
Like wise men from the East? —
Yea, surely! Could we see indeed
Our Lady in her hour of need;
The Blessed Mother, glorified,
Above this cradle-side,
Would not our hearts receive their sight,
And we go glad this night?

Ah, dearest, could we but have known
The days Love came unto His own!—
His one reproach no more but this,—
'Thou gavest Me no kiss.'
    [*He turns towards* ASSUNTA]
Bring we our treasure, and no less.
So shall it be that for her cold
And want, and sorrow, sevenfold,
She shall have more than heart can hold
    Of blessedness.
Love make our offerings to her,
Gold, and frankincense and myrrh!
    [*He beckons first to the* CHILDREN, *who go up one by one, with their gifts,* BIMBO *and* BIMBA *speaking, the others dumbly following; all watched with rapt interest by the neighbors craning their necks.*

BIMBO

I have a cricket here for mine!
I caught it, last Ascension Day;
And I gave it grass, and drops of wine.—
And when it rubs its wings
Together,—then it sings!
And I made this cage for him, out of rushes;
And it 's just like our thrush's! . . .

Holy Bambino'll love to play
With that in heaven, some day!
[ASSUNTA *receives it, smiling faintly*]

BIMBA
[*offering her plaited basket*]

O holy Francis, — I mean . . . O Blessed
  Mother!
That boy was Bimbo . . . and I'm just the
  other.
This one I made, Madonna, this one here!
And I began it long ago, — last year.
And Granddam made it too, at harvest-moon;
But I finished it again, this afternoon.

[*The other children follow, proffering their
  gifts.
The Brothers tie white goose-wings to the
  shoulders of* BIMBO *and* BIMBA, *who beam
  with pride in their angelhood. Their grandmother explains to* OLD LUCREZIA.

THE DYER'S WIFE
— The finest white goose feathers!

THE FURRIER'S WIFE
— Fine, I vow!

The Dyer

— My boy Gentile ought to see them now!
[Lucia *advances first of the maidens, with a bright scarf.*

Bimbo
[*calling out*]

Take care it's nice, Lucia, what you bring!
We're angels now; — we can see everything!

Lucia
[*humbly to* Assunta]

Lady, this kerchief for your neck, . . .
The best I have. — It is not worn at all.
Saving it was I, for the festival
Of the three Kings. . . .
The best of all my things.
Lady, I pray you, wear it, to make fine.

Other Girls

— And mine!
— And mine!
— And mine!
[*They flock towards* Assunta, *and touched with new awe as they approach, offer their ribbons and withdraw softly.*

LUCREZIA
[*listening with smiling blindness*]
And is it our maidens? — What are they doing,
Softly as doves? . . . All feathers, . . . all cooing!
> [*Beckoned by* FRANCIS, THE BAKER *hobbles up on his cane, with a loaf under each arm and a bulging pocket. There is the same homely warmth with the gift, and awe at the group before him, as he explains his offering.*

THE BAKER
Lady, Madonna, . . . think no scorn;
I kneaded and baked since I was born. —
Milk-white loaves, and both for you. . . .
> [*Fumbling in his pockets*]

Something for Holy Joseph, too. —
Eggs of the silk-worm! There's a beginning: —
Once ye have them hatched and spinning,
Each of them in his own cocoon, —
Eh, — eh? Ye know? — Ye can learn all soon.
> [*Starts to go and turns back, feeling in the other pocket.*

Ehi, I am old in the wits, look you!
Here are three slips of mulberry, too;

Ripe to set. — If ye had no more,
'T would help to keep the wolf from the door!
Blessing and Hail! — And so, farewell; —
Go safe, with glorious Gabriel!

THE DYER'S WIFE
[*to* LUCREZIA]

Listen to him!

LUCREZIA
[*laughing with pleasure*]

Old neighbor, — you? . . .
And his voice all shining over with dew!
 [FRANCIS *beckons to* THE POTTER, *who
  wipes his forehead and approaches with
  his gift; looking about, awe-struck, on the
  Manger and the group.*

THE POTTER
[*crossing himself*]

Was it like this? Was it like this?
Hay in the stable? . . . Lady of Bliss!
 [*Humbly offers his bowl, holding it up also
  for* JOSEPH'S *inspection.*

The Wolf of Gubbio

Madonna, 't is a little bowl;
Yet masterly made, and whole.
Look you, and it is lipped both ways; —
One side for hunger; one for praise.
Good measure it will hold!
Eh? . . .
I would not have it scrawled and scrolled;
The very way —   [*Checking himself.*
No, no, . . . look here,
Burnished and bright, and fountain-clear,
My ruddy glaze! [*Polishing it with his sleeve.*
And, woman dear,
   [*Fumbling in his cloak for a small bowl*]
For Him . . . and in His name, ye wit,
     [*Pointing to the Manger*]
A little fine one, like to it;
If he be found again . . . Ah, well!
Misericordia! Who can tell?
    [Assunta *is agitated*]
Holy Joseph . . . I wish ye well.

The Dyer
[*to his wife*]
Now you, Giannina, you can speak for two.

His Wife

No, you go first. No, I will, and then you!
   [*They go up together, towards* Assunta]
Madam, I . . . here!   [*Presenting her linen.*
. . . I wove it with these hands;
As any one can see that understands.
And it's fair linen, one can tell, — the best;
And from the finest flax I ever dressed!
And here's the border, and it's all for you.

The Dyer
[*with his offering*]
— And this one, too . . .

His Wife

Dyed with the purest saffron!

The Dyer

— Precious blue!

The Wife

The goodliest color . . .

The Dyer

— Ay, the blue's our pride.

His Wife

There's but a little left, of all inside —
And it will last you fourscore years and ten!
> [*She chokes with human emotion at sight of the empty Manger;—so does* The Dyer, *as they turn away.*
. . . . And then —

The Dyer

. . . . . And then,
You'll hand it down. —

His Wife

—'T will last you all your life!
> [*She vainly tries to keep him from speaking*]

The Dyer

— Yes, iron-strong, each one . . .
And you will hand them down, unto your son.—
Well, well, if not your son then, to his wife!
> [*She leads him away*]
What ails thee, woman?

His Wife
> [*weeping*]
. . . . Oh!

The Dyer

. . . . . . Whatever's at her?
Spilling out tears and chatter?

His Wife

Thou blundering man — '*Hand down*' — Oh! Oh!
The babe, that will be perished in the snow!

The Wolf

[*with a moan from his covert*]

Deh, — Guai, Guai!

[VECCHIO VECCHIO *and* GRILLO, *still cowed, look across at* THE WOLF, *while others follow* THE DYER *and* HIS WIFE *with their homely offerings.*

Grillo

— What? —

Vecchio Vecchio

'T is a dog.

Grillo

No; 't is the same . . .
The Wolf, — I care not. — [*Dully.*

The Wolf of Gubbio

Vecchio Vecchio

. . . . . . Spent, or lame,
He is; none heeds him. Look you, — tame!

Grillo

Ay, it is he . . . And he is sad,
Even as a man; or charmed, . . or mad.
[The Furrier *and* His Wife *step forward with beaming satisfaction.*

The Furrier

Madonna Virgin — [*To his wife.*] Nay, let me!

His Wife

Man, hold it up, so all can see.

The Furrier

Ecco! —
[*Displaying a large fur hood with many tails*]

Neighbors

— Ah! ah! —
But that is rare!

The Furrier's Wife

. . . . There!
Wrought with most cunning . . .

4 THE WOLF OF GUBBIO

THE FURRIER

              . . . Finest vair!
Eh? Parti-colored, — out and in;
Matched of the softest squirrel-skin.

HIS WIFE

— And set about with all these tails!

THE FURRIER

Soft as the breath of nightingales . . .
Soft as a new-born . . .

HIS WIFE

. . . . Nay now, . . . hush!

THE FURRIER
    [*looking at the Manger*]

Soft as a . . . . . thrush!
And, Lady, look you . . . if you should
Find him again, but if you could —

HIS WIFE

— Nay, 't is too large for that, this hood!
[*Leading him back; he turns and calls over
  his shoulder.*

The Furrier

But if he be lost, as they have said,—
Why, ye might sell it then, instead!

The Dyer's Wife
[aside]

Ah, furs will never warm the dead.
[Francis *comes down himself, and leads* Old Lucrezia *tenderly, towards the Manger. She seems to feel her way by the warmth and light, and reaches her arms out, her face filled with beatitude.*

Lucrezia

Look down, Madonna. — If it be
Thy will to make an old heart glad,
Shine upon me. . . .
Beautiful sons I had;
Beautiful daughters. — All are gone;
And the daylight, that shone.
Ay, all their sweetness, it is cold . . .
And I am very old.
But this I take my comfort in,
Madonna, where I sit and spin;
Dreaming I ever make
White things, for thy dear sake . . .

And for thy blessed Son . . .
> [*Offering a little garment blindly*]

See, Lady, it is done.
> [*She approaches the Manger and touches the edge.*

And was it so, the Holiest lay?
Even as a lamb, among the hay?

FRANCIS

Yea, Mother, even so.

LUCREZIA

Ah, could I only touch, and know!
Ah, she will think no scorn,
If I but feel, who never saw,—
How warm He lay, the Babe new-born,
Warm bowered in the straw! . . .
> [*She gropes, with a worshipping face, about the Manger. Suddenly her face clouds with pain.* ASSUNTA *and* GIUSEPPE *are shaken with irrepressible grief.*

Ah!— It is empty.   [ASSUNTA *weeps.*

FRANCIS
[*soothingly*]

. . . . . . Till we find
That which is lost. Nay,—

LUCREZIA
...... I am blind!

BIMBO *and* BIMBA
— Madonna's weeping!

OTHERS
[*dismayed*]
             Weeping! Oh,
What an ill omen!

FRANCIS
. . . . Nay, not so.
The tears of this Our Lady here
Shall haply wash our poor eyes clear.
Only her holy grief, maybe,
        Could make us see!
For had we cherished, yesterday,
These two that fared their lonely way, —
Had we but kept this Mother here,
Even as Our Lady dear, —
Nor sent her, as a scattered leaf,
Not caring whitherward, nor how, —
We should not stand all shamefast now,
        Before her grief.

But she who hath, for some high grace,
Madonna's tears upon her face, —
Even to us who wrought her pain,
Will she not give us wondrously,
Out of Our Lady's treasury
Pardon and peace, again?
[Assunta *recovers herself and looks up, smiling;* Giuseppe *strokes her shoulder, and looks up likewise.*

The Dyer's Wife
Ay now, he says it and it's true, too!

The Furrier's Wife
And some of it for me and you too!
For if we'd kept them here that day
When Nicolo sent them all away
So they were robbed in the woods there, maybe—

The Dyer's Wife
They would never have lost their baby!

The Baker
— Then we'd have had the Holy Bambino!
Nicolo's fault. —

The Wolf of Gubbio

Lucia
But how could he know? —

> [Nicolo *bears and protests. The murmur springs up, while others are passing before the Manger.*

Lucia
[*To* The Dyer's Wife]
Look at your two little angels there,
In the goose-wings they're fit to wear!
— Were they not telling they heard a cry?

The Furrier
— Did ever they search for the babe, put by?

The Furrier's Wife
— Search? Not they! Would they try to find —

Lucia
— Running with never a look behind!

The Dyer's Wife
Say as you will . . . From last to first,
We're all but sinners.

LUCIA

. . . . We're not the worst!
Who would call it a mortal sin,
To clear out all comers, out of the Inn?—
Were we not told, to take and prepare
And make all ready and fine and fair,
And empty and splendid for these French knights?—
And a great lord with them, that none did know,
Coming to lodge in Gubbio,
And to see the sights?—
And if they never had come then, maybe
Those two wouldn't have lost the baby!

THE POTTER
[*piping up again*]

Then we'd have had the Holy Bambino!
— Nicolo's fault!

NICOLO *and* LUCIA
[*at bay*]

. . . . . But how could we know?

Juniper

[*who has been paying his homage to the group, and ever watching the live-stock with expectancy; he points to the Ox*]

See, Brother Francis, how he looks and hears!—
And Brother little Ass . . . he turns his ears.
Will they not speak?
To comfort this our Lady, for the tears
Upon her cheek?

Children

Oh, will he speak? Oh, will he speak?

Nicolo

[*desperately*]

No! No!—He will not speak! Father Francis, sweet little father Francis,—God forbid that my Ox should turn and speak! Miracles, miracles enough, can there not be?—with sheep and birds and little fishes?—but that mine Ox should turn out to be no Ox at all?—Whatever could I do now, if he spoke? —Me walking after him at the plough, and he talking back to me! . . . What would he be saying to me?—What would he be saying?— What good would it do, what good would it do any man here if he spoke? — What would my shame be, ever after, — putting him under the yoke?

Neighbors

What's happened to Nicolo? Is he singing?

Nicolo
[*irately*]

Singing! — I? — It's the simple truth I am telling you. Say no more, blessed Francis, — Brother Juniper! You have not to say a word. — And listen, Our Lady, turn not aside. —
. . . . . . Listen, ah, do not frown!
[*Moved at himself*]
Listen, Madonna, — Oh, Holy Child! —
 . . . My heart is upside-down.
For was I not saving the space, now?
And were we not all to give place, now? —
Stable and inn, — and bed and board
For these noble men coming from France, —
. . . . Ay, and their lord?
Now hearken you two, — and hearken all! —
You shall take of the goodliest of my stall;
To be your comfort and your stay; —
[*Nigh weeping*]

Finer there is not, no, palfrey nor pony!
Take, and take home, — and ride him away : —
Pantaleone!   [*Pointing to the Ass.*
Pantaleone, — my donkey there;
      [*The people stirred to enthusiasm*]
So mild, and nimble, and sage and fair;
Yes, and his bridle too, beside ; —
Ah, what will you? — Now you shall ride
As the Holy Ones fled into Egypt, they say
      and they sing, —
From Herod the King!

Neighbors

Bravo! Bravo! Bravo Nicolo! —
— Not that a donkey is as good as a child,
but a fine donkey it is, too! — Ah, *Evviva
Pantaleone!*
      [Louis *advances with a golden casket in his
      hands.*

Louis

My fellow-pilgrims, ye have heard
Nicolo's word.
How all mischances here that be,
Befell . . . because of me :
Unwitting how my too much state
Would dispossess the desolate.

Lady, I have no gift to bring
Worthy the most high King.
Well do I see, in gold too late,
There is no kind of mirth.—
It is no more but yellow earth.
Yet, tho' I may not see thy tears consoled,
Yet, I beseech thee take
This offering for Love's sake,
Not weighed in gold.
  [*She bears with grave sweetness; the people murmur, and stretch their necks to see.*

The People

—Look, look, his offering!
—It might be from a King,
—What is it?—
                 — What but gold?
—She weeps!
         — And yet, 't is gold.
—Ah, who could be consoled?—

The Wolf
[moaning apart]
Deh! Lasso,— Guai,— Guai!
  [The King *and his men withdraw;* Assunta *is clearly seen, looking out with wide eyes of grief above the gold casket, motionless.*

THE WOLF OF GUBBIO

THE DYER'S WIFE
—Ah, how could she forget?

THE BAKER
[*pityingly*]
— Madonna's weeping yet.

> [GRILLO *starts toward the Manger as one in a trance.* VECCHIO VECCHIO *seeks to stay him, then falls back, under the same spell.*

GRILLO
[*vacantly*]
Madonna . . . I know not . . . what to say.

> [ASSUNTA *looks at him; and her eyes widen as she recognizes him.* GIUSEPPE *lifts his head too, and his face grows tense; both are rigid, with the awe of their sacred characters struggling against human pain.* GRILLO *speaks as a broken man, but younger.*

I was . . . a farer by this way,—
 . . . Only to-day.
Madonna . . . look you, I have sinned.
This cloak . . . that warmed you from the wind, —
> [*Holding it up*]

It was for want, and bitter lack.
I give it back. . . .
> [*He turns and comes down.* Brother Leo
> *receives it for her.*
>
> Vecchio Vecchio *approaches, in the same
> manner, as a man who does not care
> further what becomes of him; the people
> amazed all into silence.*

Vecchio Vecchio
[*restoring the wallet and the silver image*]
Lady, . . . I pray this grace of you;
And Holy Joseph's pardon, too.
Lady, we could not well suppose . . .
But this is truth, God knows! —
> [*Backs away, held by the eyes of* Assunta
> *and* Giuseppe, *both trembling and pale.*

Francis
Yea, she that wears in our dim sight,
Our Lady's halo, for to-night, —
Will she not see with mother-eyes,
And fold us all, — all mother-wise,
In the pitying glory of her light?
> [Assunta, *without turning her head, slowly
> crosses her arms upon her bosom and smiles*

through her tears. GIUSEPPE's *face clears into strong beauty. They stand rapt.*
LEO *and* JUNIPER, *each with a green branch, approach the Manger, and look on it with such joy and devotion, that the* CHILDREN *stretch up to see.*

BIMBA
[*calling*]
O Brother Juniper? What do you see?—
Is the Christ Child there?

JUNIPER
[*laying down his greenery with awe, almost whispering*]
. . . . . But it may be!
[*Last,* FRANCIS, *with illumined face, goes up to the Manger, and stretches his arms out over it with rapturous tenderness; —as if it were to him a bird's nest rather than an altar.*

FRANCIS
O, Nest!
Nest of all heart's desire!

Even to thee the blinded birds go seeking;
Nest of all Love!
O empty Nest, —
Be filled, be filled with these, —
The wayworn sorrows, thronging, weeping,
   thronging, —
The lost compassions, yea, the lack and longing
Without hearts-ease!
Nest that nor man nor bird did ever build,
Be filled, be filled,
Over, — above —
All our sore longing,
All our blind weeping, —
Hopeless of rest;
O Nest of the Light of the World!
Thou Nest.

THE PEOPLE
Noël, Noël!

FRANCIS
. . . . . . Nay, hark!
What heavy heart is yonder in the dark?
 [*Shading his eyes, he steps down, looking towards* THE WOLF.]
Lo, Brother Wolf!

THE WOLF OF GUBBIO

THE PEOPLE
[*looking for* THE WOLF *who is half hiding by the arcade of* LUCREZIA'S *house*]

— The Wolf, the Wolf?
.... Then he did not go?
— What, was it he then, moaning so?
— Look, is he hurt? He limps,
..... No, No!

THE WOLF
[*in a loud voice*]

Yes, it's The Wolf . . . of Gubbio!
[*Exclamations of amazement show that the people have understood him to speak in words.*

THE PEOPLE

Look, listen!— Did you hear?— Did you hear? —The Wolf's talking.—The Wolf's speaking. Is it a dream?— No, No! Look there!
—The Wolf spoke out!—He spoke a word! We heard him all — we heard! We heard!

LUCREZIA

The miracle of the flocks and herds!

190 The Wolf of Gubbio

BIMBO *and* **BIMBA**
The Wolf is talking words!

ALL
— The Wolf is talking words!

FRANCIS
Ah, Brother Wolf, thy heart was sore; —
We should have welcomed thee before.
. . . . . Forgive it, Brother mine.
Whatever burden weighs within thy breast,
Come hither, come; yea, leave it at this shrine
       That is a nest.
  [*The by-standers listen with open-mouthed
    amaze while* THE WOLF *speaks in a great
    voice of grief.*

THE WOLF
Ah, no. Lifetime is over; — past.
These words I have, are first and last.
   [*To* FRANCIS *with heart-broken yearning*]
With all my thirst . . .
With all my power, —
I strove to linger out this hour. —
Since I did live, for this one day.

The Wolf of Gubbio

This only day, when first, — ah, yes!
I heard thy words of loveliness;
Out of thy mouth; —
Out of thy heart, —
Only to-day! —
I strove . . . but could not stay apart; —
I could not creep away.
O, I was fain; — but never can
Lift me so far to be a man; —
Man the one that a Wolf would be; —
Even as thee, — even as thee!
Midnight is come; the bond is loose. —
What worth to me their stony truce?
The peace is broken, and void again,
Betwixt us beasts and men. —
So. — Let them stone, and hunt, and spurn:
Slay me! — I will not turn. —
Only to be forevermore
'Wolf-at-the-Door! — Wolf-at-the-Door!'
I have no will to live; —
Let none forgive!
All other craving is gone by.
Better to die, — than live and be
Man without love; —
. . . . . Better to die.

Francis

Nay, Brother Wolf, ah, grieve not so;
All was forgiven.

The Wolf
[*in anguish*]
     Thou dost not know
All. But thou shalt;— the one thing left:—
My gift! . . . My theft.
  [*He creeps towards* Assunta, *who looks
   back at him bewildered.*
And thou, Madonna, ah, forgive
The one long day I strove to live!
O Lady, let my heart lie there,
Even with its halting prayer
Unspoken.
I give you as I may.— My old wolf's heart
. . . Is broken.
  [*He limps with lowered head into* Lu-
   crezia's *house.*

The People

Where is he going to? . . . . . .
. . . . My way?
. . . . Your way?

See! See! . . . .
. . . Old Lucrezia's doorway!
Look at him!— Into the house unbidden!
What has he hidden?— What has he hidden?
[*Reënter* THE WOLF, *with the swaddled
Babe in his teeth. He goes up through the
crowd which parts before him,— to* AS-
SUNTA,—*and lays the Baby in the Manger.
The faces of the parents show their
amazement, incredulous hope, wild joy, as
they see that it is their own.*

THE PEOPLE

— Miracle!— Miracle!— Holy Bambino!
— Mother of Mercies!—
. . . . . And how could he know?
A man — a wolf — a man!
—No, no!—
Fra Lupone!— Fra Lupone!—
— Fra Lupone of Gubbio!

THE CHILDREN

The Christ is found! All's well!

The Knights

... Noël, ... Noël!

[*By-standers embrace* THE WOLF, *with rapture.*

FRANCIS *picks up a long green branch from the strewings, and makes as if he would play an invisible viol over his arm, singing the while.*

The Children gleefully pick up rushes in like manner, and look to him as he calls aloud for gladness.

FRANCIS

Oh, and the very stars shall sing
For joy of this glad thing.
   Lo, Love is born!
Though we crown Him yet with thorn,
Though we laugh Him all to scorn,
   Love, — Love is born!

Curtain.

Epilogue

Francis *parts the curtains and stands forth, shading his eyes, as if he were still searching the darkness beyond the tented place.*

Francis

And if there be out yonder any Wolf,
    Or great or small, behold,—
Come, little brother Wolves, come in, come
    hither,
        Out of the cold!